AF326780

Sixteen-Sixty

Life Stories

Gong Yuebin

California, USA

2021

CONTENTS

PART II.
IN CHINESE

About the Author　214

XII

ACKNOWLEDGEMENT

This book is dedicated to my mother with love and gratitude!

I am grateful to the people in my life who support and appreciate me as a person and my talent.

INTRODUCTION

For most of my visual art career, whenever I have ascended to a peak, I have always been impatient and eager to get down. I've run from the small dirt slope in my backyard to the United States, to California, my body covered in mud, yet I have never compromised. Fortunately, in the year that I know my own destiny, I can travel freely and without worries in California and Dali, can calmly watch and cultivate. Perhaps this is the beginning of a change from the first half of my life when I was "transformed by things" to "me transforming things." It is good that my heart is steady now, and I feel at ease and can finally focus all my thoughts on continuing my art profession in the second half of my life. So it is.

Gong Yuebin

May 1, 2014

California

YUEBIN GONG

PREFACE

As the pandemic evolves, my uncle Gong and I have been restricting ourselves to his house in the Bay Area while our minds roam beyond daily life: my reading and writing practices reach the imaginative cities of my interests; Gong soaks up literature and philosophy in an effort to rediscover his past sixty years. Our distinctive universes only intersect at random conversations under the sunshine of our breakfast table and in the firelight of our late-night drinks. Although I can vaguely visualize this book through our fragmented exchange of ideas, I find it hard to build the necessary frameworks for writing an appropriate preface What kind of stories does this book tell? Who could be the target audience? What ideas does this book convey? While Gong values the contrast between our minds in his invitation for me to write the prologue, I am more interested in building an alternative image of Gong's *sixteen-sixty* beyond the book's content. Instead of assembling a conventional opening for the book, I consider the following monologue a personal message toward Gong's next sixty-year journey. I also wish for this message to provide the reader with additional dimensions for the understanding of Gong's writings.

Gong has been performing a "strong figure," even as he has been a remote role model in most of my growth. This figure was reinforced by the family legend of Gong's entrepreneurship, his business success in Guangzhou and America, and my intuitive impressions upon visiting him in California. Although the figure's ambition and leadership seemed far away from my own introverted personality, my parents encouraged me to learn from him through our shared interest in art. His guidance helped me through crucial steps in my personal development, including my efforts in drawing and my decision to study abroad. However, it was not until my relocation to his house that I began to discover the true Gong, who has been making his journey under the impact of the same figure. With the help of sunshine and firelight in our daily conversation, I gradually unveiled how Gong's strong figure was shaped by his prolonged fight against society's mighty force, his journey in business and life under the figure's motivation, and his recent fear and anxiety over letting the figure down, given his persistent trauma after being involved in a drastic political strike. Gong has an idea of viewing the world as a mirror for his personal growth, and I am curious about the true self he sees, which has been covered by the layered makeup of struggling, advancing, injuring, and enduring cultural shocks, when he faces the mirror.

Over our half year of daily conversations, Gong and I have worked together to discover his true self. I attempt to articulate the social process that, over decades, shaped his strong figure, while Gong works on philosophical approaches to revisiting the origin of his personality. The process saw our familiar figure shifting toward antagonism, given his profound experience and success in monopolizing Gong's identity and values, in blocking any opportunity for additional quests. Gong's retirement from active social roles has weakened his ability to revise the figure through his mirror method. The figure appears so invincible that our attacks upon literature, philosophy, and sociology can only add to his stubbornness. To evade this figure, we eventually put our focus on Gong's sixteenth year: an age of sensing the world's dark side while not having to fight against it. This difficult era offered Gong his last luxurious moment of free will to venture before building the mighty figure. His adventures zoomed onto the peach trees of his backyard and the stage of performance in his sketchbook. Although these retrieved moments can hardly portray a comprehensive image of this era or of any gateway for Gong's escape, they can help us visualize his sincere self-expression in the face of absolute darkness. As Gong put them out piece by piece, I could see a sixteen-year-old personality emerging out of the strong figure of his current sixty-year-old form.

I do not necessarily expect this book to resemble an accurate panorama of Gong's sixteenth year, nor for it to rebuild his inner universe at the time. Instead, I see Gong's passion for retrieving the underexposed part of his sixteenth year from the shadow of his strong figure. As Gong steps into his sixties, he has taken an oath to have listening outweigh action. It not only signifies his will to rediscover the world's bright side beyond the traumas of his prolonged fight, but also declares war against the figure of his own creation. Instead of cherishing or replanting the sixteen peach trees of Gong's memorable year, I believe in the idea of retrieving his curious spirit to venture into the bamboo forest of his sixties. The questing nature of this spirit makes up my honest expectation for this book. I sincerely wish for Gong's writing to inspire and encourage his upcoming journey so that he can confidently speak out to our familiar figure: *Thank you for your support over the past sixty years. Now I shall begin venturing into the world on my own!*

Haoyu Wang, nephew of the author

January 1, 2021

PART I

IN ENGLISH

<BORN IN 1960>

I was born in 1960 [1] in a small village on the banks of the Yellow River. My birth was full of hardships; my life was full of hardships. I was like a seedling squeezed out of the shriveled earth.

People often called me a son of a bitch due to my family circumstances. I never liked this nickname. In my mind, I always thought these conflicts, these cruelties, made even the western winds of my childhood feel colder and unbearable.

God didn't seem to put much thought into the land that birthed me and raised me, either, and only made two brushstrokes, so light and transparent it was as if he were running out of ink. One stroke of blue and one stroke of yellow, this was all that made up my world. All along the banks of the Yellow River was nothing but sparse, watery dregs, the faint watercolors of the human world, like the ink

1. 1960 is one of the three years great Chinese famine.

God accidentally scattered across the barren land, little dots here and there.

Overhead the scorching sun would bake and roast the ground until the skin of Mother Earth peeled open, the flesh cracked and damaged, until all blood vessels dried and shriveled away, creating a field of uneven wrinkles and ravines in its stead. The surface of the ground resembled pieces of shortbread cut out by a knife, spread out under the sky.

The winds of my childhood were cold; the days were also cold. That stroke of blue, that smear of yellow, became aged under the onslaught of those winds, and the colors faded from the elements, weathered by the sun and rain. Slowly they changed to gray and brown, ash and mud, and then to white as winter's snows fell from the sky.

<Gong's Kiln>

Wind, whooshing past, what are you blowing? What's left to blow? The more it blows, the more desolate it gets. It's time to cease, harsh wind. The wind, coming from the west, going to the west, blows everything away. The sorrow of the poet, who inscribed 'on an ancient road in the west wind a lean horse goes,' has endured today.

Where there is a westerly wind, the horses and people are weak and thin. The people are crippled and stunted. The land here seemed to have been swept by the wind for a long, long time, blowing away layer after layer, blowing from the west to an even farther west, leaving only a thin, wasted layer of skin where nothing could grow.

Our surname is Gong. All the people here have the surname Gong and live in Gong's Kiln. It is a small village with about one hundred people on the southern Yiluo River Valley, next to the Yellow River. This surname is very rare. It was said that the name was granted by the emperor to those that left the palace. Those people, now with the last name Gong bestowed upon them, appeared and sprouted up from the land, firing up the kilns in the houses, thus the origin of the name Gong's Kiln. Kiln firing is a good way to live because, in this place, there was no other way to survive. Looking from afar, every house is dirt yellow, like the kilns. People went in and out of these kilns, their bodies covered in ash and dirt from head to toe.

My intuition tells me that this land has had a long history, long enough that people have forgotten it, long enough that people have lost their own identities. Buried in this piece of land are secrets from the past. Hidden in this barren landscape are the capitals, glorious and prosperous. It's just that people are too busy trying to survive, caught between life and death, with no time or energy to care about these mysteries.

Did the Gong family ancestors never try to leave this place? Why didn't they try to survive somewhere else? Did they never try to walk away from this desolation? I want to rediscover the identity of this land. I fall asleep thinking of all sorts of fantasies and doubts. In my dream, a grandiose and majestic caravan with robust horses and strong men slowly approaches from the other side of the Yellow River. They set up their camp here, bore and raised children here, and established themselves on top of this land. Later on, all the glories and prosperities dissipated into a pitiful state, a complete mess. Everything was blown away by the wind. Today, those that still remain here are like unearthed relics, dilapidated and crumbling away.

When the sun rises, its radiance blankets the earth. Even in this barren landscape, I can still feel God's benevolence and grace. After the sun sets, everything dims once again, giving out a few sighs. The sun and the moon continue to shine upon this land, their light filled with reverence and piety. I still have many wishes.

I long to learn, to progress and grow. I love running on mountain ridges, listening to the howling of winds. Whenever I ran on top of those high ridges, I told myself to make every step faster, and then even faster. The wind rushed into my ears, as if I could really hear something in the breeze. East wind blows green; south wind brings warmth; north wind brings snow; west wind brings desolation. Every wind has its own story to tell.

Children dream of adolescent dreams and can't care for anything else. Which child is not naive? Is there a child who does not like to dream? But during my childhood, there were never enough storytellers to tell me stories.

<Heavy Wind Blows>

The wind comes, like a wicked person entering the village, flipping heaven and earth, sweeping through so brutally it's as if the village was looted and pillaged until not a grain of sand remained.

The wind comes, and the whole village holds its breath and listens to it howling. What is on the earth's surface is blown up into the sky, and what is in the sky is blown down to the earth. Heaven becomes earth; the earth becomes Heaven. People walk backward, and their eyes have to look backward. People walk with lowered heads, as if the wind had snapped their necks. The wind, which has grown the facial features of an evil person, is omnipotent and can even turn a corner to chase people. When the wind comes, it's impossible to take a single step or move an inch and impossible to dodge or escape. If there was anyone walking on a road, they would either be blown to the right or blown to the left; on one road there would be people fallen on both sides. If people were trapped in the wind, they would stand up only to be blown down; stand up again, only to be blown down again; it would be better to lie down on the spot, except lying down doesn't work either, as the wind will send you to the horizon, to the ends of the earth.

The wind blew and brought out many "sicknesses" in people. Some could not stand the wind and were blown into oblivion until not even a shadow or a trace of the person remained. Some people, with one breeze, caught the "wind disease" and fell onto the ground, never to get back up. Some people got blown by the wind and caught the illness and fevers of madmen. Father was blown by the wind and caught dementia. He became silent, always with his head lowered, and would at times suddenly laugh and suddenly cry. Some people were blown by the wind until their lives were blown into utter destruction, ruined and destitute. Mother had also been blown down by the wind, but fortunately she stood back up. She had had her feet bound before, and they were just barely longer than the three inches of the desirable "lotus feet." When the wind came, she would grit her teeth in perseverance, tightly gripping the thick, sturdy ground, more stubborn than the wind regardless of how hard it blew. When the wind saw her like this, it could only walk away with its tail between its legs. I often saw her walking against the strong wind, one step at a time, with her body lowered toward the ground. People here either lower their head or stoop at their waist.

The wind is a single strand of thread, stringing together the past, present, and future, connecting Heaven, earth, and people. When the wind withdraws, the past and the present break apart and scatter into pieces on the ground to become stories. When the wind blows again, it connects the stories together into sheets. Sometimes the wind would thread through the pages and narrate the stories, and I would watch and listen. Gong's Kiln is like a large jar that was blown down by the wind, broken into gravel and pieces of ceramic, and scattered into every corner and crack in that place.

Sometimes, the wind blows at the sun until its face is covered in dust, filth, and grime, leaving it dirty and dimmed, without its beautiful brilliance. Sometimes, the wind blows at clouds until it disperses them. The clouds used to be round and thick, but the wind blew them into silk threads, strands, so thin they scatter and vanish in the sky. Some people lost their corners and edges after getting blown by the wind and became round and plump. Some people, after getting blown by the wind, became sharp as a knife's edge. Every time I see their evil, vicious faces, I think they probably became twisted like that because of the wind.

18

<HOME>

The light of dusk fades, slowly, gradually, and finally even the last shimmering ray has been drawn away. The sky and earth have become turbid, with more darkness than light. The canopy is still blue, but it is a mixture of dark blue created by indigo and a single drop of black ink. It is a blue with height and depth; it is a blue that enshrines the brightest star in the sky. The old tree on top of the roof no longer has any leaves, only dried branches like the hands of an enchanted ghost, stretching aimlessly in the dark blue sky, giving a sense of unspeakable grotesque. The light in my home has not yet turned on, and yet my grandfather's light in the house in front of ours has already been lit.

These dim, yellow lights are the star in front of every family's door. I moved a chair over to where the lights could reach and began my homework.

My grandfather calls me "Sharpie." "Sharpie" is my nickname. Sometimes they call me "Third Sharpie." I have two older brothers, and I am the youngest of all my siblings.

For a long time, I just agreed to everything with a "hm" and never lifted my head.

In the village, people often called me a "counterrevolutionary son of a bitch," and I became accustomed to this title. I never argued, never resisted, and rarely answered; I was always cautious and solemn, used to walking around with my head down and stuttering. I was never really close or affectionate with my grandfather and therefore was used to being quiet. He would get angry when I did not respond to him. "Little brat, so rude. You don't even answer your grandpa anymore! Your father went crazy; you are also stupid and demented." After a while, he realized he was shouting at himself all along, as I am his flesh and blood, his kin.

One day after school, the moment I walked in, I saw my second brother kneeling in the living room. I asked him, "Why are you on the floor?"

"Let him say it himself!" Mother's fierce voice severely shocked me. My brother had his head lowered, teary eyed and mumbling, his expression full of frustration and hesitation. It looked like he had gotten into trouble again. My eldest brother and older sister were preparing for middle school and were well behaved. I was still young, just beginning to understand things, and naturally was not a troublemaker; however, my second brother, who was neither too young nor too old, was at the age of an explorative tween and earned my mother's wrath every few days. In little things, I was smarter than him; however, he was better than I was in school. I could read between the lines, and I knew how to get on people's good sides. My second brother was simple and honest, coarser and gruffer, without much in the way of street smarts. What I knew was retreat, tranquility, how to balance out my parents. What happened was that our chicken had died, and my mother had cooked it, separated the legs out so that they could be presented to the village head as a "favor" to see if our village could establish a program so that children who were preschool age could begin receiving education. My mother was about to take those chicken legs to run the errand when my second brother secretly took a bite of the leg without asking anyone. You couldn't blame him, though, as everyone was desperately hungry back then and meat was precious.

My mother said this proposal was for the public's benefit as well as for our own self reasons. My mother worked as a teacher in another village a few miles away from home. On weekdays, she could not leave her classes and could only come back home on the weekends. I was not of age yet for first grade in elementary school. My father was politically designated as right-wing and was therefore forced into physical labor to work in the Production Team, tending the pigs. He was timid and could not stand the political attacks, his mind was becoming abnormal, and all day long he was just a yes-man. My mother often asked him to look after me, to which he would shake his head and utter, "No, no, no, I cannot." Mother pitied all the kids left in the wild without a care and, more importantly, worried about there being no school for me. Her proposal finally received attention and action from the village, and thus kids like me were able to receive care before reaching school age.

My mother's name is Li Yunsheng; she was born in 1923 and graduated the Luoyang Provisional Girls Middle School. She was a lady from a rich house in Luoyang Liuli village. Her father was part of a noble family within a radius of a hundred miles. Due to a colleague's jealousy and plot, her father died when she was fifteen. Mother had an eye disease after birth, leaving her with only one functional eye her entire life. Even though she was born into a landholding family in the feudal era, she was not enticed by riches or makeup but had a passion for education. She went on a hunger strike when her family did not agree with her going to school. Finally, she became one of the few educated women during that time.

My father was named Gong Shangzhi. He was born in 1920 and graduated from Yian'an Lu Xun Normal University. In 1938, he joined the revolution after being taken by underground revolutionaries for education in Yian'an. He worked for the Yian Qing Department of Education. After returning to Luoyang and marrying my mother, he worked together with her in the city as a teacher. In 1959, both of them were designated as right-wing and were sent to the countryside for re-education.

After my father's political attack, he was in a perpetual state of waking and dreaming, of being worried and scared. He frequently talked to himself and laughed from time to time, and in later years, he spoke even less and just smoked. Often, he would be smoking at the front door while my mother was washing clothes. Mother would try to persuade him, "Please stop smoking. You are making your health worse," to which my father would reply, "I have nothing else but this smoke. If smoking is gone, I will die." After hearing that, Mother said, "Then you should smoke less." For my father's suffering, it would have been better if he was able to cry everything out.

Later, Mother's official job was restored, and she became a teacher in the countryside. The most familiar scene of my mother's return on the weekends: She would always walk hurriedly from the front yard to the backyard, and just after stepping through the front door, she would begin to unbutton and take off her coat, as she rolled up her sleeves and entered the kitchen. Inside and out, she could always find "things to do." The house was only alive when she was present. Even though she only had vision in one eye, she was never fuzzy in life; even though she had bound feet, she had never fallen. She always had her ways around the family.

"Teacher Li, sorry, could we borrow some flour? The kids at home are growing and eat too much. When the team sends food, I will return it to you," the neighboring lady said to my mother, standing at the door. Mother did not hesitate. She immediately went into the kitchen and grabbed a bowl of flour. The lady gave a word of thanks and left. Mother was always generous toward our neighbors, but in my memory, she never borrowed a single grain of rice from others regardless of the tough situation at home. This was not about saving face, but about mentality. Mother never indulged us and would rather have us eat worse-quality meals so that food could last longer. She would never allow us to have a full stomach after only one or two meals in exchange for scraps of food later on. Every holiday, all the kids from different families in the community would gather together and show off their delicious meals, but I never dared to bring out my food because my bowl was so shabby. My father said, "Your mom always makes food like monks do, mixing sand in the rice," but whenever my dad could speak a few clear words, I was always excited.

Whenever the Production Team distributed food, our bag of flour was much smaller than the others. I asked my mother why we got the least when we had so many family members. She told me that the flour would be harder to carry if there was too much. Later on, she told me the real reason was that she could only receive a salary from working as a teacher and no work points. Our food was distributed by regulation while other families got not only the regular portion, but also extras redeemed from work points; thus they always had more food than us. Mother mixed the white flour with sweet potato flour so that while the surface of a bun would be a thin layer of white flour, the inside would be mostly black sweet potato flour. Only during New Year's could we eat buns made of pure white flour—smoky, heavy, fluffy like a snowball, and pure like a cloud. I heard milk has a similar whiteness, but had never tried it before.

Our family did not fit in the village. Villagers often said that we were uptight. However, I did not quite understand for what we were considered uptight. We did not swear, did not curse at others, nor did we fight back when cursed at. Those who are teachers teach; those who go to school study. The entire family was quiet. Every night that my mother was home, after dinner, in order to save oil, she would only light up one oil lamp on the living room table where everyone gathered around, reading books, writing, and doing other tasks. There was only the sound of pages turning and pens writing. I have brothers and sisters, in total five siblings, but we only had one or two lights. Wherever the light touches, people will gather. At that time, people who didn't pay attention to life were richer than those who did. Having knowledge is to have dignity while life is poverty.

Once, Mother went to my grandma's home to get some food. From what I heard it was my aunt secretly sending assistance to the family because she wanted to hide it from my cousin. There was no trace of Mother even though she had been gone for more than two hours. It turned dark outside, and everyone began to worry as they were waiting in the house. My eldest brother proposed that we all get a cart and go outside to receive her. As we were traveling downhill, there was a person sitting on the ground crying as they looked up into the sky, or maybe it was the hills in the distance. There was a sense of hopelessness and despair. It was Mother, with two bags of food next to her. She had been thinking about her past when she was a jewel in a privileged, noble family, and about how she had ended up in her current life due to her stubbornness and unwillingness to compromise. The situation was beyond the gods' reach. In the midst of all that sorrow, she cried. I rarely saw Mother shed tears.

Everyone worked together, pushing and pulling the cart, continuing on the journey home. My elder brother was very strong, pulling the cart from the front while everyone else pushed from behind. I ran alongside and cried when I could no longer run. Mother picked me up and put me onto the cart. I sat up high on the cart, enjoying the view and feeling happy, my face beaming with a smile. My eldest brother slapped me across my head when he saw me laugh. I instantly didn't dare to make any noise, pouting but still feeling secretly happy inside. As we climbed uphill, everyone had run out of strength. The sky was turning dark, and the road was becoming fuzzy, and in an instant the cart tilted and the food tragically poured out again. I almost fell out of the cart as well, but my mother grabbed me with one hand, stopping me from falling into a well next to the road as I was right over the edge. My mother gripped me tightly. Finally, when we almost made it home, food poured out again. Again, the tragedy replayed, and again, we all cried.

When we arrived home, Father had been waiting for us with

the light that he started. When people are there, the light is bright. Light originally is fire, and after it is covered, it becomes light. Home originally is a house, and when people gather together, it becomes home.

28

<AFTER SCHOOL>

"Brat, finished school? Are you going to be looking after the pigs like your father? I do not think you will do well because pigs run faster than you," a few villagers said to me as they sat on rock slabs, smoking and conversing. They would tease me every time I passed by. I grabbed my backpack, silently running toward my home.

These people cannot be left with free time to idle away. In the fields they cannot put down their hoe; in life they cannot let go of the alluring but smelly stench of money. I know they cannot let go of their poverty.

My family often became the topic of discussion: "This family has so many members but so few are working. What does it matter if they have imperial exam candidates and scholars? How long have they lived off it? Still their fortune has perished. Prosperity truly never lasts more than three generations! It just so happens that Gong scholars have reached exactly three generations."

I was very timid and evasive in the village, due to their glances as well as idle gossip and slander. When I was in third grade, my mother was assigned back to Gong's Kiln as a teacher. After that, I walked to and from school with my mother at my side every day, and thus felt much more relaxed.

In those years, every household raised two or three pigs. Every day, the pigs had to be "assembled" in the Production Team's pigsty so that all their excrement could be collected and used as fertilizer for the fields. The school was right next to the pigsty. Every day at noon, when the bell rang, the kids would get out of school, and the pigs would get out of their sty. Students and pigs all rushed out together. There were the heads of people, the heads of pigs, all heading off in the same direction, with people walking upright and pigs walking horizontally. When the students saw all the pigs, they were amused and began running, shouting, laughing, and chasing after them. The pigs could not stand the ruckus, and one would start to run away, causing everyone to lose their heads and start running. Soon chaos ensued, with pigs pushing and shoving past each other. There were people running into people, pigs running into pigs, people running into pigs; there were people chasing and pigs running, people laughing while pigs were calling; there were pigs following other pigs, gasping for air.

One pig ran after another pig, their butts sticking out, tails curling, holding up their white-and-pink bodies with four snowy-white legs. When they ran, the lump of meat hanging over their stomachs shook back and forth. Those short legs started from thick to thin, then tapered to sharp edges at the ends, finally tiptoeing on their hooves like fat ladies wearing high heels, every step a little graceful and a little strenuous. The pigs' feet were short and thick, but even though they were small, they were tough. As the pigs ran forward, their feet trod the ground and raised layers of dust. On top of their heads were two fanlike ears that waved about in the wind, as if the pig was confused. As the pig ran, it began to panic and become anxious, losing its way, losing its sense of direction, and without knowing how, it ended up in front of someone else's house. Once it saw that it wasn't at its home, with an expression of puzzlement and bewilderment, it would leave without a single farewell, only making two noises of "*hmph, hmph*" inside its throat before turning around and leaving.

Even if the pigs make mistakes, they will eventually find their way of returning to their homes.

32

<OPERA>

I can no longer recall the last time I watched opera. When I was about seven or eight years old, an opera troupe came to our village to perform. Rows of stools were laid in front of the stage, patiently waiting for the show to begin.

The stage setup produced a light show, with rays of red, yellow, blue, and green. Amid the desolation, these bits of red, bits of yellow, bits of green were a grand scene to us children. The colors in this desolate village were truly bitter, as well as bland. This little bit of light allowed people to momentarily escape from the taste of bitterness. With the actor's long robes and beard, as well as the several types of stage paint blossoming on his face, it was hard to know whether he was laughing or crying, to know if he sang of happiness as if it were a tragedy or sang of tragedy as if it were joyous. Opera is like life; you can never perceive the truth within. The people offstage don't care if the actor is crying or laughing, if they're sad or happy; they're only focused on clapping and cheering. This is what it means to watch an opera.

I sat in a corner offstage, my loneliness reflected in the single shadow next to me. From afar, a single soul, I watched children my age laughing, shouting, running, and making a ruckus onstage. I knew them; they were all children of the brigade cadre. They were well dressed, neat, clever, and witty. When they laughed, their laughter was released unobstructed. The entire stage was filled with their laughter and joy, to the envy and admiration of all watching. In my heart I felt lonely and wanted to get onstage, but I understood that I did not qualify, I didn't have the right to. The first dream in my life was to become the son of a brigade group branch secretary.

I took out the sketchbook hidden in my cotton-padded jacket and furiously started drawing what I saw. I looked at the stage, and it looked back at me. Unfortunately, the battalion commander of the brigade militia walked in front of me then, displaying an aura of unfriendliness, like I had done something criminal. I lifted my head to look up at him and felt anxious in that moment. He looked at me silently and looked down at my sketch. I didn't want him to look and attempted to hide it with my hands, which was the moment he grabbed it from me, flipping through it, looking at it, and ridiculed me with a sneer: "You are drawing? What is it? You think you have the right to draw? Go pee and look at the reflection; an antirevolutionary son of a bitch like you has the right to draw?!" After he finished, he tore the sketchbook to shreds and threw it on the ground, pointing at me while berating me loudly and swearing at me while walking away. I picked up the broken sketchbook from the ground; I was not angry, just panicked and feeling a little wronged. I wanted to go home, but the opera was about to begin. Should I go home or watch? Never mind, let's just go home.

At the time, I did not understand opera and even more so did not have the opportunity to go up on stage. But inexplicably I suffered through a villainous play, and the stage in my heart collapsed. What I didn't expect was that the show offstage would be even more funny and absurd than the one onstage. That wicked person and the nightmare that came with him naturally wouldn't be onstage because only the made-up scenes presented there. That giant curtain was solemn, straightforward, and righteous, as if to tell people something.

From then on, every time I watched the opera, this scene came to mind. Inexplicably, the show no longer felt interesting.

<Sweet Potato>

Every year at the seasonal harvest, in front every house lies pieces of freshly unearthed sweet potatoes, still holding on to the vine, like a newborn baby who has not yet had the umbilical cord cut; stained with mud, smelling of fresh mud after being uprooted, lying on the ground, breathing. Just like this, it was born from the ground, with a dazed and confused appearance, not knowing where to go.

Boiled sweet potato, steamed sweet potato, roasted sweet potato, dried sweet potato, sweet potato flour, sweet potato noodles, sweet potato soup. . . I ate it every day and every year for eighteen years. Life continues; sweet potato continues. When it enters the mouth, it sticks to the tongue and sticks to the throat. It looks silly with the skin on and looks silly with the skin peeled off. In cold weather, the sweet potato exudes steam, and so does my mouth. You eat it one bite at a time, and eat it calmly, because sweet potato cannot be eaten too fast; otherwise it will burn the intestine and block the blood.

From my birth to the age of eighteen, sweet potatoes were the only food in my childhood. I grew up eating sweet potatoes. In addition to sweet and salty, my tongue only recognizes one flavor: sweet potato flavor. There was no chance to taste other flavors at that time. Pieces of sweet potatoes were stashed in the cellar at home, piled up like a mountain, as if telling me that life would be buried under sweet potatoes. How wonderful would it be if those sweet potatoes turned into a pile of white flour?

Every day when I walked out of the school gate, the students and the pigs had a fight, mostly due to hunger. People were hungry and pigs were hungry. They went back to their respective homes, eating the same sweet potato, but experienced different flavors. The entire village was inundated by the familiar sweet potato flavor.

"Mom," I said as I took off my backpack, "Mom, what are we eating today?" Even though I knew it was sweet potatoes, I couldn't help but ask, hoping to have a surprise when I opened the lid.

"There is sweet potato in the pot. Eat it while it is hot!" she answered.

The sweet steam came out from the lid, heading directly to the nose. The ripe sweet potatoes lay in the pot with their skin cracked, and I didn't know if they were crying or laughing. They were short and clumsy, some with skin cracked, revealing the yellow flesh inside. Those that stuck to the pot were almost burned to a crisp, with the bottom of the pot covered in a layer of dark sweet potatoes' syrup. The one piece I picked was sticking to the pot, unwilling to come out. I licked the sugary juice on the sweet potato with my tongue. Sweet potatoes are sweet and soft. However, when people are hungry, their mouths crave saltiness.

"Mom, where are the pickles?"

"They are gone. Wait a few days; your brother took the last bite." The sweet potato was peeled and tasted bland, but what could I do besides eat it? Finally, I peeled them, broke them apart, and placed them in a bowl and used a chopstick to crush them, mash them, and then added salt. I looked over to my mom and then added a little oil, turning them into mashed potatoes, yellow and soft. With oil and salt, it tasted different. I thought that if you added a little bit of green onions and garlic, it would look like the peach orchard on the small dirt hill in my backyard.

I still didn't feel satisfied. After finishing the mashed sweet potatoes, I was only 60 percent full. I saw that the fire under the stove was still burning, so I threw in two raw sweet potatoes and buried them under charcoal fire. After about ten minutes, the sweet aroma came out. It was black as the charcoal, with smoke still lingering on the skin and sparks on both ends of the sweet potato. I peeled the roasted sweet potato in two—it was hot! The skin was burnt, but the flesh was tender. Ah! So sweet.

I looked to see if there was any more sugar left in the can. After opening it, I saw that there was only the empty jar. I shook it vigorously, and some sugar crumbs came out. With a spoon, I scraped the sugar residue on the side of the jar, which came out to half a spoonful. I pinched the sugar with my thumb and index finger and sprinkled them over the roasted sweet potato. Sugar fell like snow. Ah! My world was snowing! A piece of sweet potato was covered with snow, appearing much more refined. Many years later it became a sweet memory.

Sweet potato can make people feel numb. The tongue becomes numb, the eyes become numb, the numbness from an unwillingness to change, and the numbness from an unwillingness to resist. How can we save ourselves in these long and poor days? Only by changing the way you eat can you bring out an assortment of flavors and bring out the taste of injustice.

When I look back at the days accompanied by sweet potatoes, it was a total of eighteen years. The tongue and stomach are already engrained in my memories. The taste of sweet potato can be retrieved with just the sight of them. Today I laugh at myself for looking like a sweet potato, like its outside appearance, dazed, dumb, and clumsy. The heart is also like a sweet potato, crispy and refreshing when raw; soft and hot when cooked. One has to be like a sweet potato. You must be able to endure being steamed, endure being roasted, endure being fried, endured being flattened. The most important thing is to know how to turn yourself over and turn your life around.

<EATING SALTED VEGETABLES>

The days I had salted vegetables were unique. When they go down the throat, they can suppress hunger and fill up the stomach. With salted vegetables, a meal became more substantial. With salted vegetables, even sweet potatoes have the taste of meat. Mother always said, "You guys should eat less; they are expensive."

There was a jar of salted vegetables at home. The jar was big and there were few pieces of vegetables, so it was never enough. There was a once-proud radish, now chopped, pickled, lifeless, wilting. Over time, the bright colors and roundness were lost. But when it was time to eat, these pickles that were always served in a small saucer, that lofty air and dignified manner, that essence, vitality, and spirit that comes after being freed from oppression, able to see the light again, looked so much more refined and exquisite, even more refined and precious than meat. Why pickles are so tasty, it's hard to explain. Perhaps it lies in its taste—salty. The so-called "flavor" is nothing but a heavy, strong salt flavor. It's strange that this very salty thing is still hard to forget, and the mouth is always greedy for it. After eating the pickles, you will feel a little full; otherwise, the stomach will always be empty. In short, every meal of pickles is a meal of pleasure.

One day, my second brother and I were having "rice" at home. This so-called "rice" was sweet potato with pickles. We held the sweet potato in our left hands and the pickle in our right. The right hand was busier. You had to pinch a piece, small and dainty-like, and send it to your mouth—crunch—and then pinch another piece and send it to your mouth—crunch. So crisp! It smelled so good! In addition to enjoying the taste of pickles, you can also enjoy the crisp sounds from your mouth. My second brother and I were very happy, knowing in our hearts who eats more and who chews louder. The sweet potato was forgotten, left steaming in the left hand. In the room, the two of us kept crunching.

My mother yelled from the kitchen: "Don't keep eating pickles! Three bites of sweet potatoes with one pickle. Who eats it like that? You're going to eat us out of house and home! I bought it the other day, but we're all out today." We didn't dare argue and started eating sweet potatoes obediently. My second brother was at first dumbfounded and didn't dare to eat. He glanced at our mother. In the end, he couldn't help but go all out. He picked up a piece of pickled vegetable and stuffed it into his mouth. He bit down—crunch. This invited another round of mother's heavy scolding. I listened, silently, and stuffed pickles in my mouth calmly, one piece, two pieces, three pieces, first without biting, and then a bite of sweet potato, and then I let the sweet potato wrap around the pickle in my mouth, chewing slowly. Although the mouth is not honest, the sweet potato is honest and makes no sound, and it even knew how to protect me. This way I got to eat a lot and didn't get scolded by my mother. All I did was change the way I ate, and I escaped my mother's hearing.

I often felt guilty for my cleverness and felt sympathy for my second brother who didn't understand the looks and silent hints of adults. As I chewed the pickled vegetables and looked at the sweet potatoes in the bowl, without my knowing why, the pickled vegetables in my mouth gave a burst of sour flavor at the end.

<SIXTEEN PEACH TREES>

There was a small soil slope around my backyard with sixteen small peach trees planted on it. Under the sky, these sixteen peach trees had canopies full of branches and leaves, and they joined together to protect me and became my sky, allowing me to sprinkle joy into them. It was okay if others don't understand it, even though I can't say what I did inside, but once I was there, I could stay there for a long time, half a day even. I counted many times; it was sixteen trees, and these sixteen peach trees were the garden of my childhood.

In spring, the branches were peachy pink. This color belongs only to peaches; other plants cannot grow such beautiful colors. The pink is dotted on long, thin branches with overlapping stamens. Although they are gorgeous, they are not vulgar, and even if they are vulgar, they are vulgar and pleasing. Some are in full bloom and open to the sky; when they are open, they laugh and laugh in the spring breeze. The sky is an expanse of blue, and the peach blossoms under the blue sky are one flower bud, one stem, one bunch, one tree, sixteen trees. Above my head was blue, covering the entire sky; below that was red, clusters and clusters of red. They contrasted with each other, after mating. Red retreated and gave birth to green. The leaves were slender and green, and the peaches were round and green. Although the leaves were lush and luxuriant, children's eyes are naturally sharp and can find round fruits at a glance. Ripe peaches can't be covered, and there will always be traces of ripeness. The peaches with red amid the green are the best. After the passing of spring, summer, and autumn, the ground would be covered with falling leaves. The northern wind would blow, turning the brown branches into cold, snowy brambles. When the north wind blew again, some snow would fall and some snow remained, hanging from the branches. Through the numerous and complicated four seasons, under the numerous and complicated peach trees, was a tiny, little me, quiet and unmoving.

This peach orchard was my world. There was not a single bit of threat, not a single bit of sorrow; everything was in its heyday, its prime. Maybe it was because I was small and afraid of being bullied outside; I couldn't help but care for these sixteen small peach trees that were thin and weak like me. Toward a peach tree about my own age, I was very serious, so serious, for fear that they were going hungry, and I was even more afraid that they would die. They were my heaven, my paradise. In the orchard, I was the master, not a slave, and furthermore, not the son of a bitch. In there, you don't have to be sensible; you don't have to be obedient; you don't have to suffer through people's stares. Rolling, climbing trees, digging soil, weeding, reading, painting, catching bugs, anything goes. Grown-ups always said that I was clever, lovable, well behaved, good at playing and not disturbing people. Since they said that, I became even more behaved. I also have impishness inside, but my "impishness" was reserved, and not exceptional. There was once that I fell from a peach tree, but it only hurt a little of my skin and flesh. My eldest brother, without distinguishing between black and white, gave me a beating without asking. I just felt wronged. In this family, I was my mother's darling. No one dared to do anything to me. Only my elder brother beat me. I felt wronged and couldn't understand; why did he not only not comfort me, but actually give me a beating? I thought perhaps it was just because he was my elder brother.

That winter, I went out to "skate" with a few friends in the village. Unexpectedly, the ice surface of the ditch hadn't completely frozen yet, and it was not strong enough. As soon as the person walking in front stepped on the ice, the ice broke, and one little friend fell into the ice hole. One of my feet got stuck in the ice, too, and I almost stumbled. Fortunately, the ditch was not deep. Everyone worked together to pull us up, pulling out people and pulling out our urges to cause mischief. We were cold and worried about getting a beating when we went home; as we walked, we wondered what to do. I suggested going back to my house to the peach orchard in my backyard. The peach orchard in the backyard was my meeting place, our safe haven, our harbor. In there, sixteen peach trees helped us stand guard, and we could use the firewood my father had collected to dry our pants. Three sets of wet trouser legs were roasted over the fire. The trouser legs were breathing and smoking. Someone, I couldn't tell who, asked, "Has your dick been roasted yet?"

In the midsummer of that year, seeing that the peaches were almost ripe, I was hasty to pick them from the tree, put them in my vest, and give them to my mother to be praised for my efforts. As a result, my body was covered in peach hair, and I became a monkey. My skin was itchy, and my clothes had to be taken off while still filled with peaches. I was completely stripped naked and took a bath. It was the first time I knew that even these round and soft peaches actually had a way to bully me.

My peach orchard was my peaceful, quiet, tiny world. The trees heard all, saw all, and above all, always knew me.

On three sides of the peach orchard was a bunch of small dirt slopes. Right above those slopes were dirt walls that were used in the past as the village walls, as stockades. These thick and sturdy walls surrounded the backyard. From a distance, it looked like a mountain ridge, erect and towering high above. I often ran on it alone, was able to stand tall on it and look far into the distance. The wind on the mountain ridge was strong, the sky was vast, and the ground was boundless. After being exposed to the elements as wind and rain, the small soil slope gradually collapsed on both sides and wasn't as high as before, but I was now much taller. When it rained heavily, the rainwater drilled into the soil on the small slope, carving out deep trenches. The soil on the slope slowly loosened, and chunks of it flowed down with the water on both sides. I rushed to the soil slope, lay down flat on the ground, stomach pressing tightly to the earth, and used my whole body to press down on the earth and protect it from the rain, letting the rain hit me instead. I wanted to protect this place that, in my heart, was a piece of Pure Land, of Paradise, and my homeland. I couldn't bear to watch these dirt walls collapsing, and I couldn't bear to watch this perfectly good mound of earth henceforth being scattered and broken apart. My house was already dilapidated enough; I couldn't let these sixteen small peach trees, which were surrounded by this small dirt slope, be ruined as well.

Little did I know, the nightmare was yet to come. One day, a few people from the Production Team came to visit, saying that the brigade needed to burn kilns, needed firewood, and all these trees needed to be chopped down. They were members of the brigade, operating under the name of the brigade, and they even brought an ax, so there was no room for negotiation. In my heart I was panicking and frightened, so dumbstruck I was simultaneously anxious and crying. When my mother saw me crying and railing against the heavens for the first time, she was heartbroken for me.

Embarrassed, she begged them: "Could you wait until next year to cut down these trees?" Even though I knew that the brigade was too important to turn away and that their orders were irreversible, for my sake, my mother still put aside her pride and pleaded on my behalf. As I watched every moment the ax fell upon every peach tree, I clung to my mother's back, simultaneously crying and feeling the trees' pain and suffering. It had been so difficult for them to grow up, and it had taken so long to grow this field of peach blossoms, but they still couldn't resist the chop of the ax. In less than two hours, the backyard was too appalling to look at, a terrible and tragic battlefield. I felt like I had watched this whole scene while dreaming.

Everything was gone. The trees had fallen, the sky was empty, the ground was empty, and my heart was empty. I had cried myself to exhaustion and now stood foolishly in a daze on the side. I had lost everything, had nothing now, so I didn't need to worry about losing anything anymore. From that moment on, I had no more best friends, no one to protect me. As I thought of them being burned to ash, it was like Heaven and Earth were being torn apart, a last farewell. As I stood there on the now empty spot, I cried again for a while at the leftover, broken young branches. I sobbed as I picked them up and asked my mother, "Mom, can these branches be planted?" My mother, taking pity on me, replied, "My son, don't cry. Next year I'll plant new peach trees for you."

The year after this, my mother really planted sixteen peach

trees. I visited them every day, several times a day. I wonder if they had taken root, but you can't dig through the soil to look. At that time, I didn't feel like eating, didn't feel like meeting people, and even when it came to studying, my heart wasn't in it. I floated through life in a daze, in a state of bewilderment; dimly, when I thought of the sixteen little peach trees I had lost, there were tears in the corners of my eyes, which dripped onto my pillow. In my dreams, I saw again those sixteen peach trees. Suddenly I felt like urinating. I took off my pants and faced them, drip, drip, drip. . . Hurry up and grow, my little peach trees.

A child's heart has always been an acre of farmland, and planted on that land are a child's dreams. I often rejoice that my childhood was awakened and built by these sixteen peach trees. Although in the end I lost them, for all the days to come, I was able to pick up the fragments of those memories to create many more dreams. My compassion, my innocence, and my vigor are all because of them. I always chased the memories of the sorrows and joys of my childhood, and alongside all this is the outpouring of love that accompanies these memories. A piece of desolation wrapped around a little piece of this peach orchard, a little piece of this peach orchard wrapped around a little boy, and a little boy was wrapped around a peach-shaped heart. These sixteen peach trees allowed me to accumulate endless potential. This potential should have another name; it's romance. Sixteen small peach trees keep me forever young at the age of sixteen.

<SUCH A YOUNGSTER>

As the decade moves forward, as the days continue to waver and linger, I grow.

Once my hands and feet became long, my clothes became short. The sleeves became 80 percent as long as before, my trousers now reached above my calf, the soles of my shoes had worn thin, and my toes were about to come out. There were many patches on my clothes, pants, and schoolbags. The patches looked like stitches over wounds. Looking at them, it still hurts. The color of the thread is the same as the color of the clothes and pants, but some are different and look like they are ridden with scars. The color of the clothes were mostly the colors of bitterness: gray, indigo, black. Among the bitterness there were some hints of personality, perhaps toughness. I don't know where it came from; perhaps it popped out of the ground. Within my eyes flow determination and tenacity, from within my eyes burst forth beams of light, consequently making this era of my life appear more glorious. The soles of cloth shoes were not tough, but people's feet are very tough, and they can always churn the dust off the ground. They carried red flags, blew whistles, beat gongs and drums, held their heads high, shouted slogans, and rushed to open up a new world. They looked high-spirited and passionate, but I've always disliked fanatics and zealots.

I looked very flat at the time, just like old clothes, stitched and mended, and after putting on the worn clothes, my appearance became even more wilted. Hunger often attacked me, approaching step by step; I had to tighten my belt. Hunger is difficult to describe, as long as the individual understands it. The demands of hunger are unstoppable, and one can only follow it unchecked, with abandon. The hunger of adults is different from the hunger of children. Adults can escape from the prison of hunger as long as they turn on their sides. A child's hunger is a threat that tightly chokes you. At home, my younger sister was hungry and cried from time to time. When she cried, I quickly fed her sweet potato and rice soup. I was also very young, but I couldn't cry anymore, even though I was still a child. Ever since I started the first grade, I was responsible for picking her up from the kindergarten, letting her ride piggyback to school and back home. You could say it was one child carrying another child piggyback.

In a flash, I became a sixth grader. One day after class, a female classmate drew a picture on the blackboard. I can't remember what she drew. I stood by the blackboard and drew according to what she drew. When she saw me imitating her painting on the sidelines, she immediately picked up the eraser and erased her painting. What! Was she angry? Maybe. I continued to draw from memory. Fortunately, Mr. Li, the head teacher, came in, and I was standing in front of the blackboard holding the chalk. He looked at the drawing on the blackboard and was taken aback, then looked at me. He could not believe the drawing on the blackboard came from me. The head teacher at the time was my favorite teacher; his name was Li Xin. He taught both Chinese and the fine arts. In my opinion, he was really "new," and there was not a trace of being old-fashioned within him. His "newness," like the feeling of wind and light, made people want to approach him. With excitement and surprise, he asked me when I learned to paint and how long I had been learning. He praised me for painting well. I was in a panic mode and didn't dare to breathe. I froze there and didn't dare to swallow my saliva.

I whispered, "Teacher, I have never learned to paint. I painted following that female classmate." I pointed at her but didn't dare to look at her.

The teacher went on to say, "The National Day is approaching, and every class needs to publish a poster. You will be responsible for the National Day poster masthead of this issue."

When I heard it, I was flustered and didn't know what to do. I was so excited but also worried that I could not do well and would let down the teacher. I wanted to avoid this assignment but didn't dare to; instead, I just said I would try.

I went back to my seat in a daze, pretending to be listening, but my mind was still on what had happened, replaying it again and again in my heart. Though I received the girl's scolding, I won the teacher's attention and praise. I thought, If it wasn't for her... I was constantly speculating, one hypothesis after another, which were then disproven and overturned. Sometimes a little light, sometimes a little heavy, all the while my mind was in a state of confusion and disorder. Everything came too quickly, and it was overwhelming. It happened because of her, but I didn't know if I should be grateful or apologetic and definitely did not dare to look at her. The outspokenness and recalcitrance of girls, the ignorance and confusion of boys, it happens in every generation, the game of body language and speaking through your eyes. Boys are inexplicably shunned and treated with indifference by girls; even bullying and ridicule are a kind of attention, and they secretly give birth to shame, happiness, and throbbing feelings in the heart. Every time I think about it, it's the same.

The summer night enveloped the earth. People returned home; birds returned to their nests; there were still some stray flying insects and wind. Some stars hung in the night sky. All nights in the world are similar. The earth is always desolate, and the river always rushing. After dinner, the old man waved a fan outside the house to cool himself; naughty boys carried kerosene lamps to catch frogs and throw themselves around in the darkness. Only one or two lights were on in the entirety of Gong's Kiln, waiting for everyone to fall asleep. I was still in the classroom and didn't go home.

In the gloomy classroom, you can't see if the night sky has more stars or less stars, and you can't hear the sounds of insects flying and frogs croaking. A dim yellow kerosene lamp flashed slightly. The teenager stood shirtless on the stool, and the stool would sway from side to side with any slight movement. He tiptoed up slightly, and his trousers followed the movement up, exposing his ankle. Holding a paintbrush in his hand and stretching his arms, his shirt would hang above his belly button, revealing a flat waist and the top of his trousers. He forgot the time, forgot hunger and thirst, forgot the darkness and viciousness of the night, forgot the infestation of mosquitoes and let them suck the flesh and blood on his back. His entire body was stuffed in the steaming heat, sweating constantly; the beads of sweat accumulating between his upper lip and the tip of his nose were slightly salty. The darkness of the night could never suppress the brightness of the light; the darker it was, the brighter they were. The kerosene lamp has always been fragile and sensitive. A little wind will make it jump and swing, going in and out. That night, it burned silently, very well behaved and very quiet; as if it were being encouraged, the flames burned higher and higher. In the middle of the night, the flame was a little less excited and calmed down and became a little sleepy. In the second half of the night, I was getting in the groove; my sweat gradually disappeared, and I began to feel proud and cool.

A classroom, a teenager, and a lamp have become a scene of light and shadow; the light of the kerosene lamp is similar to the moon, illuminating the night and making it more like night, illuminating the silence and making it more silent, illuminating people into greater focus, and illuminating the emptiness of the classroom. That weak light was not so spread out; it was only on by my side, and the rest was dim and dusky. The light illuminated the gloom, illuminated the backdrop of a tween boy. Like a blessing, the light is blessing the piety and sincerity of the moment, blessing this tranquil painting, full of Rembrandt-style light and shadow; a sculpture in honor of Michelangelo, displaying the power of Michelangelo's genesis. But this is just in hindsight. Who knew Rembrandt back then? Who was Michelangelo? Who can appreciate the embarrassment and misery of kerosene lamps? A twelve or thirteen-year-old boy, his hands and feet and body are as thin as branches, without a trace of sensuality. The skeleton penetrates a thin layer of skin, a groove in the middle of the back, a flat waist, and a belly button as small as an unopened eye. These are all things I was unaware of. And when I learned to paint later on, I never made this "self-portrait." This is also hindsight.

I stayed in this position for more than ten hours, as if I was tangled up and suspended by invisible strings. I was there from six in the afternoon to the early morning of the next day. I got off the stool and let go of the breath I was holding in my chest. My spirit returned to my body, my whole body recovered, and my blood slowly recovered, only to realize that my hands were sore and numb, and my stomach was empty and rumbling. Looking back, in that empty classroom, there were only these uniform rows of tables and chairs that kept me company all night. I blew out the kerosene lamp, and a puff of acrid and pungent hot kerosene gas rushed toward me, and I inhaled it. The sky was already bright with sunlight, and when I opened the door of the classroom, the cool morning breeze blew over me, and I heard the cheers of the birds, and there was a glimmer of red on the horizon, the dawn of a new day. I ran toward the house, livelier than ever.

When she saw me return, my mother was very happy and waved a fan for me. She looked at me intently, smiled, and said that my two nostrils were black. I picked up the towel, wetted it, and spread it on my face. It was so cool and refreshing. I dug into my nostrils and looked at it. Sure enough, the towel had two small, black, round holes! I laughed too. Breakfast that day was the same as any other day—still sweet potatoes, but sweeter than before, maybe because I was hungry. Because I was eating too fast, I couldn't get it up or down, and I choked as it got stuck in my throat. I walked straight to the bucket, took a scoop of water, drank a few mouthful, stayed still for a few seconds, and it finally passed after a few hiccups. I was a little too excited. It was as if my body couldn't seem to wake up, and after painting all night long, while still a little tired and dizzy, I hurried back to school.

My mother said that she came to the classroom several times that night and looked at me secretly through the crack in the door. Even her steps were gentle for fear of scaring me. Through the light, she saw mosquitoes on my arms and back. She felt anxious and distressed but couldn't bear to disturb me; she was in a dilemma and didn't know what to do.

This was the first time in my life that I "did something" and felt the joy of accomplishment. I was waiting for things to happen, and I also looked forward to the teacher's viewing of my poster.

Teacher Li pushed open the door of the classroom and with one glance saw the masthead on the wall. Instantly, his expression was that of disbelief. I remember he was very excited, and while I was waiting for his excitement, he spoke to me in a very serious and severe tone: "I want to tell your mother." My mother was also a teacher at the Li family village school. The teachers all knew my mother and knew me as the child of "Teacher Li." My teacher's tone was firm and decisive, as if the situation was urgent and needed immediate action. He called the school leaders and teachers over, praised me and the masthead I drew, and then advertised to other teachers that this board newspaper's masthead was drawn by a student who had never painted before.

I stood to the side, silent. They nodded, smiled, and turned their heads from time to time to look at me and then to look at the masthead. Some people said, "This kid has never learned to paint, such is the young surpassing the old." Some said he didn't even have anyone in front of him to learn from before he had already surpassed. Some people said that Teacher Li's children were different and well educated. Some said that this kid was gifted, talented, and it would be a pity for him to not learn to paint. Their voices drowned me.

This was the first time in my life that I received attention, respect, and recognition, and the person who discovered me and my talent was a teacher I respected, a "new" teacher. I was so used to being scolded that this moment made me uneasy, and on the contrary, I felt apologetic and regretful that I wouldn't be worthy of this praise. In the eyes of my neighbors, I was nothing but an "anti-revolutionary son of a bitch." This sudden change in fortune, my life turning over a new leaf, left me at a loss. From that day on, I forgave the desolation and tragedy of the westerly wind; forgave the irresistible hunger; forgave a lot of the crooked, twisted, and slanderous faces; forgave the tragedy that befell the sixteen little peach trees for no reason; and forgave a lot, so much.

Next, the teacher gave me an important task: to complete the school's National Day propaganda masthead, in only one week. There was no need to go to class. Just like that, I spent a week in the principal's office, from first being careful to later carefree; from the unfamiliar to the familiar; in and out, out and in. Mixing colors, paint; mixing colors again, paint; one picture a day, a total of six pictures, and the last day was for my rest. The content of the masthead was mostly Tiananmen Square, the national flag and national emblem, a red star, red scarf, a red lantern, a pine tree, and so on. Later, everywhere I looked I saw Tiananmen Square, the national flag, and the red star. A week later, the whole school, village, and Production Team were circulating that "the child of Teacher Li's family is a little painter and a little genius." During that time, I felt like I was burning like wildfire. I didn't know where the wind came from, but once the spark was lit, everything had gone out of control, like an unstoppable prairie fire. I was at a loss, and I didn't know what to do. Prior to this, everything I dealt with was all "kid stuff," and I was always ignorant and muddled. Suddenly a beam of light lit up my body; this light seemed to pull me out of the dusty, forgotten corner of fate.

From then on, I was addicted to painting, drawing everything that could be drawn until the sky was dim. My objects to draw were as large as the sky, land, rivers, mountains, villages, houses, people, and as small as pots, pans, clothes, shoes, hats, kettles, flowers, birds, trees, insects. Painting after painting after painting. Knowing, not knowing, seeing, and imagining. To

paint is to "move" living objects onto the painting book,

with my eyes and hands becoming the moving company. The hands are painting while my eyes are constantly moving and capturing the image. Sometimes, the eyes can see clearly, but the hands are not satisfactory, and the drawing does not turn out well. Sometimes, the eyes are half open, but the hands are very determined, and the result is unexpectedly good. For example, to draw a tree, suppose you want to "move" the tree into a painting book. In the past, once the trunk, branches, and leaves were painted, the drawing was done. Later on, though, I compared it and found something was off, or wrong. Was that tree tall? Short? Slim? Strong? Old? Younger? Leafy? Still bald and lacking leaves? Had it grown longer toward the west or east? What were its emotions? Its story? and so on. A single tree was enough for me to ponder for a long time. After thinking it through, my hand proceeded. The eyes must be sharp, and the hands must be quick. If the painting was ugly, I felt apologetic to the tree. When the painting was rough, it was like completing only half of the work, cutting corners and taking shortcuts. For example, when I would paint a cloud, I would think about the cloud's swift movements, the melancholy of the cloud, the cloud on a sunny day, the cloud on a cloudy day; I would think about how sometimes the cloud is high and the sky is wide, but sometimes the cloud is dark, overwhelming, and oppressive. Was the cloud looking down at the world of humans or dreaming with closed eyes? Did it want to stay or leave? Looking at the cloud in the sky and the cloud in my painting book, it seemed that they were not the same cloud. The cloud under the pen looked like a heavy pile of shit. When this was the case, I was afraid the cloud would really be angry. Another example: If there was a person wearing a flowery coat, how should I draw these clothes on their body, and how should I draw the flowers onto the clothes? When I took a look, I found the person in the painting had no clothes, but instead had flowers growing from their body and stretching all around, almost covering and submerging the figure. I didn't know what to do, and it was embarrassing. A lively bird could alight on my painting and cease to fly, as if it was stuck in the air. In my drawing book, people seemed to collapse and become flat. The sky looked square, but it's not really square; the earth was round, but not really round. The tides in the gulf, the towering mountains, the scenery. . . I drew cautiously and solemnly, carefully, with crooked and straight lines, swaying circles, and within every painting was a staggering, stumbling self.

I enjoy doing things quietly; I am unwilling to make noise and disturb others. At that time, I was young and didn't understand the thought of "If you don't talk, you can be an instant success." It was only later that I understood that that night would become every night in my future. My life also changed drastically because of that night. There was not much thunder in the north, and even in summer, thunder is rarely heard. After that, I watched what I was watching, dormant in the world and biding my time, with only a pair of longing, thirsty eyes, hidden and buried away. Other people naturally didn't know anything about me.

67

<Walking Out through the Mountain Gate>

Gong's Kiln is like a jar, surrounded by a wall with only one opening. This opening is the mountain gate. The gate actually has no door. It is a gate rammed with soil, about four or five meters high, and the inner wall is about two meters thick. It was hollowed out to form an arched door. There were not many people coming in and out of the mountain gate, only one every few days. There is poverty inside the gate, and the road leads into the city after passing through the mountain gate.

At that time, you had to look the part when going out the door to the city and then change your appearance when coming in the door. At that time, I was young, and apart from wanting to be the son of a party secretary, I had a wish to go out through the mountain gate and enter the city.

Before I was born, my parents were both teachers and taught in the city. In 1959, they were labeled as rightists and sent to the countryside for reform. To be able to walk out through the mountain gate and return to the city had become the dream of my family. My longing for the city stemmed out of a child's curiosity. At that time, I was not mature or sensible; I just wanted to go to the city to see something new, like the road and the train. After leaving the village, you could boast and show off in front of your companions. For Mother, she knew too well what she was responsible for and what she was looking forward to, and it was for her children to walk out through the mountain gate one by one.

When I was in the fifth grade of elementary school, my eldest sister met a person who was from the city. Later on, he became my brother-in-law. With this relationship from the city, the family naturally became different. There is a glimmer of hope after one enters the city. My brother-in-law was the only city person in our family and the first person to take me to the city. The first time I entered the city was like a dream. When we are small and young, how can a person's eyes contain an entire city? The appearance of the city is: many people, many cars, and many lights; a road, ten meters wide, jet black, straight, without curves. Some people go on the left, and some people go on the right, walking smoothly. After walking around the city for a day, there was no dirt on my shoes. For the first time, I felt that there was no hurry to get home.

On the day I came back from the city, the villagers looked at me steadily, as if they didn't know me. Those who come back from the city can't restrain their joy. They show off inadvertently after a trip to the city and make it known to everyone. People gathered around and asked me about the city. In the past, I was a "grandson" in front of them, talking and stuttering. After returning from the city, I became a "grandpa" and spoke a lot more fluently. I shook my body, fixed my eyes, and told them that the road in the city was "Glass Road." The ground was transparent, shiny, and smooth like glass. When they heard it, they felt amazed. They stopped talking and were silent, looking at the ground in a daze. And then they asked about other things. I told them that the train was so fast, as fast as a rocket. As I described it, I pointed at the sky. Everyone followed the direction of my finger and looked toward the sky, as if looking for a train in the sky. I also told them I watched a movie. When they heard it, they jumped up with excitement, and they had me act out a movie for them. I promised I would and got a flashlight from my house, pulled out a handful of dog's-tail grass from the ground, and took them to a dark place in my house. I held the flashlight in one hand and shone it on the dark wall. In the other hand, I made the dog's-tail grass shake under the light, and the shadow of the grass fell on the wall. This was the "movie." Everyone cheered and clapped their hands continuously. After that, I gained some "reputation."

I can't recall how long it had been since I went to the city, but I had matured by the time I heard that my brother-in-law was coming to take me into the city again this week. The second time I entered the city and was going to stay there for several days. I was so excited that I didn't sleep all night. This time, I was determined to look more carefully and truthfully.

A building was a building, people were people, cars were cars; there was no dust; it was clean and neat. The city was very noisy, mostly the sound of cars coming and going. I was still going to see the train. The train was still the largest and longest car. I thought it was gone, but there it was still, continuous, very long, longer than I thought—boom, boom—sticking to the ground and moving forward; its segments, broken but connected, too fast to see clearly. It would be nice to live near the train and see the train passing by every day. When I grew up, I wanted to take the train and ride back and forth. Was the train manned or unmanned? Was the railway straight or curved? Would the train turn? Did it know how to turn around? Did the train's brakes work?

After that, my brother-in-law took me to the Cultural Palace, which was a new world that I had never seen before. There were many kinds of paintings in the Cultural Palace. Of these kinds there were: Chinese paintings, oil paintings, sketches, and figure paintings. Sketches were divided into body sketches and still-life sketches. The paintings seemed to be real. These proficient painting skills impacted me. Facing this sudden influx of artistic nourishment, I watched closely, wanting to engrave every painting into my mind. I'd been dry for a long time, any rain and dew that I found would make me greedily absorb it. It wasn't until my brother-in-law called me three times to leave before I walked out of the Palace of Culture. We went into the Xinhua Bookstore, and the books smelled good. The books were neatly arranged in rows, layer by layer. Perhaps I was too excited, like I was dreaming. I was in a daze with no idea where I went and what I saw. I just remember that my brother-in-law bought me some art books and painting utensils. I was so excited that I stayed up all night and touched them all night.

After living in the city for a few days, I saw that the people in the city looked like they lived in the city; in other words, they had a city lifestyle: undressing out of dirty clothes, changing their shoes, hanging up their hats, washing their faces, gargling with mouthwash. People in the city didn't speak so anxiously, so loudly, and they talked slowly so that they could be heard clearly and comfortably. You must have proper manners when you eat in the city, and you can't make a sound while picking up food. My brother-in-law was very good to me, but I was afraid of the new place and dared not to talk nonsense. If anyone asked me anything, I would answer. If they didn't ask or say anything to me, I would stay quiet. As I looked around, I found people in the city would always have a way to place themselves and everything in their lives. Is this what they call mindfulness and propriety? There were rules for eating and rules for sitting. In the living room, shoes were placed in the shoe cabinet and feet were placed in slippers. In the kitchen, there were tableware and chopsticks in the cupboard. People were polite and used to saying, "Thank you."

When I returned from the city, the city air was still floating around me, bright and beautiful. I walked on the road, and I had no time thinking about what I was thinking, and had no time to take people's glances into consideration. It was probably because of the paintings exhibited in the Cultural Palace, which shocked me and made me excited and flustered. I wanted to stay in the city for a few more days to see more deeply and more carefully. On the other hand, I wanted to hurry back and face my own painting. I was a little conflicted and a little frustrated. Back at home, I hid in my room and played back the bits and pieces of those days over and over again. Gradually I put aside the excitement of watching the train in my mind, only staying focused on the paintings of the Cultural Palace and what I saw and heard with the lifestyle of the people in the city, scene by scene, over and over again. I was a frog at the bottom of the well. Gong's Kiln and the Li family village were just small wells. Thinking of this, I was secretly sad. The melancholy and sadness that I felt in the past were nothing, but when I thought about it, they were really inexplicable. I couldn't tell what to dig out of my heart, what to eliminate, and I felt a little confused. Looking up at the sky, I was sure that I was different, and the sky was different. My instinct told me that this time that I was out of town, this experience, was preparing me for everything that would happen in the future.

Back home, I decided to make a pair of slippers for myself. First, I found a peeled and broken belt. I cut the belt into two segments a bit wider than the forefoot. I cut two planks, equal to the length of my feet, and cut them into almost the shape of my feet and smoothed them all around. I got a few nails and used a hammer to nail the belt to the left and right sides of the board. Now it was just right! I made one for each side. A pair of slippers, it's done! I tried it, and it was a good fit, but I walked a bit stiff, like I was wearing Japanese clogs. It was not that slippers were not suitable for me, but that my feet were not suited to slippers. Looking at my pair of handmade slippers, I was secretly joyful. The two slippers were like two small boats. After putting on the slippers, I started looking at my feet. These snow-white feet were small, still growing, and the toes were like small dolls. They didn't need to be sensible. I wanted to make them playful and lively. It turns out that feet can be placed so gracefully, something I had never noticed before—so simple, yet not so simple. Life was originally flour that was so finely crushed that it could not be shaped into anything. Later, after adding water, it became sticky, and then, after constant kneading, the flour became dough, letting us shape it. Life is an act of creation. The act of creation is justified; the enjoyment is justified.

Even though I did not create slippers, my first pair of slippers was created by myself. I put on the new slippers and walked toward the door, a little shaky and shy. My grandpa and uncle happened to be sitting at the door, and when they saw me like this, they scolded me. My paraphrase of what they yelled: It didn't take long for me to come back from the city, for me to learn from the people in the city; you don't know your identity anymore; you don't know the height of the sky and your limitations, and so on. Then again: How are you going to work in the field when you're dressed like this? The two talked for a while. Let them scold; I would continue to wear my slippers, still feeling righteous. My toes were so happy. What they cursed, I didn't really care. I knew what they were thinking. A pair of slippers was extravagant at that time. People didn't even want to have extravagant desires anymore, though I believed that one day they would also wear slippers.

They thought safeguarding the old ways was stability. They especially hated people or animals that refused to stay still. They were oxymoronic; they did not like others to walk ahead of them if they could not walk farther themselves, if they could not go any farther. They were used to everything that is the status quo. Thus, they could not sit still when people disrupted these ordinary lifestyle habits.

I put the slippers under the bed, showing a sign of obedience. Whenever I arrived home, though, I would change into them right away. Life was now different. When I realized there was a pair of self-made slippers under my bed, I felt there were lights in the sky.

When I held my bowl again, I discovered a ring of black material in it, and when I pinched it with my fingers, they became black as well. Seeing the black wall behind the stoves, I realized this was smoke dust. Our home lacked a kitchen cabinet. I found a paper box and two bars of wood pellets. I put the two wooden boards on either side of the box, and with a few bricks alongside as stabilizer, the box would then be secure in between. Then, after washing, drying, and cutting the transparent plastic bag that was once used to contain fertilizer, I would attach the bag to the box as its cover. This way, no more dust would go in. Every time after the family was finished eating, clean bowls could be placed inside after opening the cabinet. Also, whenever we ate, there would be clean bowls ready to be taken out, which would make the food cleaner than ever. Even though there were only sweet potatoes in the bowl, the taste was already different than before.

By walking out of the mountain gate, by entering the city, my horizons were broadened. I remembered the things that were worth remembering in my heart, like pieces of precious treasure. I had definitely changed, but I could not make out the person I had become. It was just that now there were so many things within my mind, within me, that came from outside of the mountain gate. Maybe the others had forgotten, but I was someone who had passed through the mountain gate. Many years later, all five of my brothers and sisters also walked through the mountain gate one by one, exactly as my mother had hoped.

78

<Old House>

Every time I go back to my hometown, I feel distressed to see the vicissitudes and ruins of the old house. There are a lot of weeds on the corrugated surface, and the wind shakes it slightly. There is strangeness in the long absence, familiarity in the strangeness. Still the same plaques—"Conqueror of the Literature" and "House of Virtue"—are upright and square on the walls. This is its eternal identity, and it is also the bloodline and pulse of the Gong family. I looked at it, and it looked at me. I closed my eyes and greeted it in my heart: "The ancestors of the family, I am back." It was silent, a kind of promise. The old house is old after all. Fortunately, I can still recognize it; it naturally recognizes me.

The old house has stood for several generations; it already has an ancient and expired look to it. The appearance of the door has not changed, only grown old, age changing the color to brown, the color of wood. It's still beautiful. The lock is also old and rusty, as if locked with a story. A lot of weeds have grown around the wall, and the grass grew taller, almost flooding the old house. Upon entering the house, there is a stale smell, burying the old story. There are very few furnishings in the house, empty but for some old and unusable debris. The room was very dark, with only a few rays of light shooting down from above, and dust was visibly floating in the air. Oh, the rain broke through the tiles. Ah! I can recognize that this was my room. The outer wall had collapsed, revealing a large hole, and the blue sky can be seen. The wooden beams broke down, and the tiles and walls had collapsed into a mound. The grass outside the wall took advantage of the vacancy to enter. The sky, the wall, the grass, the old bed, I stared silently and in a daze. This used to be an oil painting: "Old House."

I like oldness, everything about oldness. I can't explain the reason. Oldness, like a fading memory, gives a sense that what's deep and profound about it has disappeared and only tenderness remains, which makes people can't help but approach it, walk into it. The color of the old house looks beautiful, only a little faded, so old it has stories. It's just, there are fewer and fewer sentimental people now, and fewer and fewer people who are willing to listen to stories. The old house is telling a story. Some stories are unclear and lost forever, never to be told. The window is broken, leaving only one window frame, and the old scenery is no more. The walls are mottled with water-stained leaks, telling the story of time. There is a chair in the middle of the main room that makes one feel old and melancholic with one look. I never forgot a single corner. When I was young, I had no one to tell me stories; instead I would look at this old house because it was a story, but I couldn't guess what story it was telling. Now, I can probably guess the story.

My family lived in the ancestral house of Gong's Kiln, a courtyard made of blue-gray bricks. My parents told me my great-grandfather was Gong Yuzhu, a first-degree scholar of the late Qing Dynasty. The "House of Virtue" hanging above the door of the house and the "Conqueror of Literature" plaque hanging in the hall were bestowed by the emperor. The plaque is mottled and dull. Although it has been weathered a lot, the traces are still clear. Before I could read and before I had started school, the first thing my mother taught me to recognize was the six big characters "House of Virtue" and "Conqueror of Literature." I often stood in front of the hall, watching and gesturing, as if looking at my great-grandfather. It seemed that he was also looking at me. Although I had never met him, I thought he must be as old-fashioned and solemn as this plaque. If my great-grandfather was still alive, he could have taught me to read and write, and he definitely would have loved me the most.

My third grandpa's family lived in the front yard, and our family lived in the back yard. My third grandpa used to be my grandfather; it's just that, since my second grandpa didn't have any children, my third grandpa adopted my dad out to him when he was young. My second grandpa passed away early, leaving our family and my grandma behind. We were at a loss, with no one and no safe harbor to turn to.

As far as my father was concerned, his adoptive father had passed away, and he was separated from his biological father. In the end, no one came to our rescue. My third grandpa was my father's biological father, so he should have been intimate and affectionate with us, but he seemed so polite it was unnatural. After the adoption, there was the feeling of separating inside his heart. Grandma thought of us as adopted family and never warmed up to us. In short, each lived in their own house, doing their own work, eating their own meals, and living separately and in peace.

"The Gong family patriarch is a fine person, and he takes good care of the folks in the village. Out of the brothers it seems the second brother is the best, but he had no fortune and was unlucky. If he had lived longer, he could still protect the family legacy. So many descendants, none of them look like Master Gong's eyebrows. The youngest little brat actually looks a bit like Master Gong when he was young, especially his mouth and manner. It looks the most alike when he doesn't speak." This is what the village people always said.

Their sympathy and sighs could not hide their enjoyment from watching this drama play out. They recounted and criticized the past glory of other people's families and today's pitiful aftermath. It was as easy as commenting on an opera, relaxed and effortless. It was a pity that the show ended and there were no more scenes to watch.

Our whole family seemed to have been abandoned by fate,

swept away by the times like dust, and given the cold shoulder and snubbed by the rest of the family like we were a bunch of old, unwanted junk cast away in a forgotten corner. An entire generation of a scholarly, intellectual, reputable, aristocratic family was like this house, gray with dust and ash, old, decrepit, and broken.

It was embarrassing, but a poor man still has his joys and delights, and no matter how poor we were, we still all celebrated the New Year. Beginning on the twenty-third day of the twelfth lunar month, the entire village became a bustling scene for the New Year. There was joy in the cold air, which, although harsh, encircled the joyous celebrations. All the kids were on break, so why shouldn't everyone hurry back? My eldest and second-eldest brothers did some repair and fine work around the house; my eldest sister was knitting sweaters beside the stove; my younger sister was reading books to study her new vocabulary. The person in the greatest hurry was still Mother. She took out all the fine and soft fabrics in the house to wash, took out the cotton wool inner padding from the bed and attached it to poles to dry, and beat it with a dough roller, once, twice, three times, up and down, left and right, inside and out. Fine and scattered dust floated in the sunlight and covered her entire body, but she didn't care; then, she scrubbed and beat the bedcovers and sheets in the water, and with every squeeze, black and gray water rushed out thickly, as if she could squeeze out her pain and grievances.

From every family's kitchen, smoke rose continuously from

morning to night, and the whole village seemed to be steaming. The neighbors who called me "a son of a bitch" on weekdays were also more kind, and the kids who normally didn't play with me also slowly got close to me. Chinese New Year is filled with hope and wishes for children: hoping for new clothes, hoping for red envelopes[1], hoping to see firecrackers, hoping for delicious food, hoping for all sorts of fun. Mother bought the cheapest pig's head and pig's trotters. With the pig's head and trotters alone, she made several sets of offerings to dedicate to our ancestors and enough meaty delicacies to celebrate the new year. On the New Year's Eve, my father was making offerings to the ancestors, my eldest brother was writing Spring Festival couplets at the Eight Immortals table, and my second brother and I were climbing up and down the ladder to paste Spring Festival couplets on the doorframe. A piece of paper with the character "Prosperous" was properly affixed to the "forehead" of the door; three small spring couplets were attached to the "chin" of the door, like three red beards, floating and singing; two more were on each side of the door, like blush on either cheek. It looked like the face of an opera singer, complete with red makeup. The old house also became new, by wearing new clothes and new makeup. My eldest sister helped Mother to cook, and my younger sister ran around everywhere, joining in on the fun.

Time to eat! New Year's Eve dinner, amid the sounds of

---

1. Red envelope: various amount of money inside. It is given to children during Chinese New Year as a good luck and prosperity.

firecrackers from far and near; the whole family had gathered around a pot of hot dumplings, eating with joy. The steam in the bowl obscured everyone's faces, and only the hazy shadows of faces could be seen. The heat made everyone's face moist, dewy, and bright, and our eyes were moist as well. One after another, fat, white dumplings, each with a little bit of meat inside, were all wrapped in mother's blessings. I wanted to swallow mine in one bite, but I couldn't because it was too hot. After I took a bite, the white dumpling skin now showed teeth marks, and there was a delicious, salty, meaty taste. After eating the dumplings one after another, and finally drinking a bowl of dumpling soup, my belly bulged out like the dumplings. My father walked out of the house, preparing to make a fire for the new year, so I followed. Although my father usually didn't do anything, New Year's Eve was his stage, and I was his little helper. That night, with my father on the watch, our home felt much more secure and stable. After the meal, my mother distributed firecrackers, candies, and lucky money to all the children in the room. Everyone put them on their bedside table, watching, counting, and guarding.

For me, the happiest thing was to be able to put on new clothes. I lay on the bed, too excited to fall asleep; dimly, I saw the fire outside the window, and it was my father keeping watch. The fire outside the window was red and bright, and the pine branches crackled and popped inside the fire. The sounds of firecrackers continuously going off came from far and near. This was a sleepless night. In my mind, many stories were drifting farther and farther away from me, until I could not tell which ones were true and which ones were imaginary. All I was thinking about was how the first meal of New Year's Day the next morning did not have to be sweet potatoes.

On the first day of the new year, when the door opens, the smell of gunpowder comes rushing in, but it is aromatic! The ground is full of firecrackers that have already exploded, leaving behind a field of red. This is the New Year. I stood outside the door, wearing new clothes, stepping onto the remnants of red on the ground, looking for some dummies that had not exploded. These dummies still had unburned gunpowder, and as long as they were opened and lit, they could emit sparks. Even this little spark would make me happy. The sound of firecrackers and fireworks came from the village, intermittently, long and short, one after another. The firecrackers of families with authority were like a big, red, round cake, and once you untied them, they unfurled into a long string, like a red snake, winding on the ground. After they were lit, this red snake seemed to be enchanted. The whole body scurried and bounced on the ground, letting off all this fire and noise. The sound when it was about to burn to the end was short and dense, and it seemed that all the power was piled up there. With a bang, the firepower rushed out, like a bomb, exploded into flowers, and ended in the sky, proclaiming their victory and their completion. Our firecrackers were always a thin "little red envelope," often controlled by my eldest or second brother, who would tear open the package, revealing the fuse, and once it was lit, throw it into the air, where it would crackle a few times and then fall on the ground. It would let off—bang, bang—a few more times, struggle a few times, and then some blue smoke would appear, then nothing more.

"Come on, go greet Grandpa on the New Year! Wish Grandpa good health, and prostrate yourself to Grandpa." Our mother took us and kneeled on the ground with her hands together, as her mouth said the blessings of the New Year.

Grandpa sat on the chair and smiled. "Good! Good! Good! Hurry and grow up to win glory for the Gong family." Grandpa gave each person a red envelope. I carefully opened my red envelope, and several cousins also opened theirs. They got two dimes in each red envelope, and my family always received one dime.

After paying homage to the ancestors of the Gong family, the door of the old house was locked. At this time, the sky was overcast; perhaps it was going to snow. My mother and I were preparing to go back to the city[2]. In Gong's Kiln, some new houses had been built. The new ones were bright, and the people who lived there were not like the vicissitudes of the past. When I met a few neighbors, they recognized

2. After the Culture Revolution ended in 1976, my mother returned to her previous teaching job. It took another ten years for my father to be cleared of wrongful accusation.

my mother and me. They invited us to sit in their home and praised Mother's ability to educate people, and said that every child she taught was talented. This was all just friendly small talk. They looked at me and said they recognized me but vaguely and could not call me by name. The neighbors who used to call me "son of a bitch" were old. People had become careful and didn't want to mention things from the past. Life had improved, people had become kinder, their anger had calmed, and they could laugh now. We exchanged simple greetings and said goodbye.

Before parting, we looked back at the old house, still as quiet as before, silently listening to us quietly come back and quietly leaving. As soon as people left, there was not much life left in the old house. I prostrate to it again in my heart, and it always silently responds to me. The old house carries the memories of my birth, my childhood, and my youth. Everywhere in the old house hides my expectations, my loss, my joys, my sorrows, my secrets, and my pursuits. Fortunately, old houses are always accompanied by old trees, and old trees will always sprout in spring and shed their leaves in the autumn. A fallen leaf gently swirled on the air and finally landed on the corner of the old house. The old house always has its place to return to.

<SO IT IS>

This year is the year to know one's destiny, and I always wanted to give myself an evaluation. At the end, I could only lightly say one line: "So it is."

On March 12, 2012, when my fourth series "Site 2801-Heavenly Inquisition" premiered at the Crocker Art Museum in California; when my work "Site 2801" and I were featured on the PBS *NewsHour* broadcast; when I got the honorary certificate issued by US Congress, the California Assembly, and the Mayor of the State Capital city; and when more than half of my works were collected and purchased. As an artist in the United States, nevertheless I couldn't get excited. I was nostalgic for when I first arrived in the United States; my heart was filled with feelings of strangeness and unfamiliarity, and I was unknowing like a blank piece of paper! I sat alone in the studio, staring at the century-old, wooden roof, at the overflowing piles of works and paintings on the wall, and at the stack of certificates and flowers that I had just brought back from the museum. It seemed that everything that occurred today resembled a big show or play that had now come to a close, but nothing happened, nothing existed in reality. The applause made me return to that young boy, attached to his sixteen peach trees and that little dirt hill. What I am most excited about is not the moment of applause, but the moments of preparation and the moment I am ready. I think this is my self-awakening; it's time to look inward.

In retrospect, for most of my art career, there has always been such a strange cycle, and it is almost always the same: whenever I have ascended to a peak, I am always impatient and eager to get down.

I remember thirty years ago, my graduation artwork "Mountain Peak" won the first prize of the Henan University students' art competition, and the work was hung in the center of the provincial art museum. Ten years later, I went to the Guangzhou Academy of Fine Arts to continue my studies, glory and triumph in each and every step. I also couldn't get excited then. I don't remember when I developed the habit of walking away from the crowd. Perhaps it was my parents' miserable and tragic political shadows and influence on my life. Or was this because of my own personality, my nature, and the limitations of my circumstances? I always like to set off alone and then return alone; I like to fly alone on mountaintops and explore canyon depths; I seem to have always been a will-o'-the-wisp, a flame that dared to be away from the earth and also was willing to return to the earth. Perhaps this is destined to be my fate.

I remember that when I was very young, other children liked to form groups and run wildly in the street. It always seemed like I could only be alone in my backyard, standing vigil to protect the world that belonged to me: a small, elongated dirt hill and a square orchard of sixteen small peach trees. Later, the sixteen little peach trees were dug up and burned by the village cadres, and the only small dirt hill that was left was often washed away by the heavy rain, little by little, together with the memories of my bitter tears that I often shed for them. That was the first time I felt loss and helplessness, and the first time I had ambition and strength. It may also have been the first time in my life that I learned all I have is my own thoughts and actions, not the glory and conflicts of the world.

All these years, every single one of my paintings, every series of work; every stirring of my heart, every inspiration I have, all have come from childhood experiences and memories and the perceptions and entanglements of my youth. I don't want to cling to the past, the present, what was acquired, what was lost, what I long for, what I spurn... Suddenly, I am a middle-aged man with white hair on both temples. It's only time that grows up, and only time that grows old, yet I am still here. In life, what is broken will stay broken; what is complete will eventually be completed; dreams that were broken before can be reforged. Whether this is a "vicious cycle" or "one act," my throttle and brake are luckily always under my feet. My feet always seem to be facing forward and forging ahead, but my heart, at every minute, at every moment, stares behind to look at the past.

In the blink of an eye, I've run from that small dirt slope to the United States, to California, my body covered in mud, yet I have never compromised. Fortunately, in this year I know my own destiny; I can travel freely and without worries in California and Dali; in the two places that have become paradise, I can calmly watch and cultivate. Perhaps this is the beginning of a change from the first half of my life when I was "transformed by things" to "me transforming things." Using the opportunity of this book's publication, I have gathered all the things I have done in the United States for the first time over the past ten years. Although it may not be proper, it is a chance for me to straighten things out. For others, I take it as if I've changed into casual attire to go out and meet my guests. It is good that my heart is steady now, and I feel at ease and can finally focus all my thoughts on continuing my art profession in the second half of my life. So it is.

Gong Yuebin

May 1, 2014

California

<SPRING BAMBOO SHOOTS>

Today is the Lantern Festival, on the fifteenth day of the first lunar month. In my memories, it was the climax of Chinese New Year during my childhood.

Without mentioning the bustle and excitement from neighbors all around us, in our village and beyond, just the boldness, grandeur, and courage of my mother's "amnesty" influenced my childhood in a way I remember to this day.

All the preparations my mother made for Chinese New Year, such as decorations and food, were all things she didn't watch too strictly on this day. Pork head meat, paired with garlic and cabbage, one could eat with big mouthfuls. The bread that was roasted until golden brown and dotted with red dots, and white steamed buns, we were allowed to indulge in until we were full. Of course, the life-saving sweet potatoes we always ate could be, on this day, shunned with disgust and ignored without an ounce of guilt or remorse. Most of all, Father would bring out on this day the family heirloom, a blue-and-white porcelain tea set that originated from the Ming Dynasty, and make a pot of Shifeng Longjing, placed on the old-fashioned, square table in the center room for the whole family to aid digestion and quench their thirst as well as satisfy their taste buds.

I always remember the Lantern Festival on the fifteenth day of the first lunar month every year. Although it is not a festival here in the United States, I am still habitually used to being busy during this holiday. The Lantern Festival in my memories is not an experience you can buy with money. As I looked at the fresh and tender bamboo shoots, just recently appearing in the market during early spring, I became determined that this year I would use the shoots to chase after the memories and nostalgic feelings of the Lantern Festivals of my childhood.

My memories regarding bamboo shoots all occurred after my childhood. The first memory was when I was sixteen and I read a section of dialogue between two characters from Honoré de Balzac's serial novel, *Les illusions perdues*. Bamboo shoots are not some sort of famous French aristocratic dish that commoners and ordinary people can afford to eat.

The second time was when I was sixty years old and lived in a bamboo forest with my art school classmate Chen Yongzhong. The place we stayed in used to be the residence of the famous artist Huang Tingjian, one of the "four masters of the Song Dynasty" in Jiujiang, Jiangxi Province. The village was called the "First Village of Chinese Scholars." A common dish for the villagers was native chicken stewed with bamboo shoots. Only at this time, living and sketching in a bamboo forest and eating bamboo shoots every day, I began to understand a little bit about the dish. The bamboo shoots are picked in the morning fog the day after the spring rain and are stewed with local chicken in a medium fire as the top grade. The first taste of the bamboo shoots is crunchy and crisp. It is not too greasy nor too plain. It has the quality of being refreshing and memorable. The character of bamboo and bamboo shoots was highly favored by the famous poet and writer Su Dongbo. He has the following insights on bamboo: "I would rather eat without meat rather than live without bamboo. Without meat, one is thin, and without bamboo, one is vulgar. Thin people can be fat, but vulgar people cannot be cured."

In fact, bamboo shoots are not only a famous dish in Balzac's novel, but also a nourishment for Zen meditation.

A spring meal with bamboo shoots stewed in chicken soup on the fifteenth day of the first lunar month, under and bathed in California sunshine, amid sweet memories, nostalgia, and new, vigorous longings and desires; this year, bamboo shoots took on the protagonist's role to round out the Chinese New Year of my memories, the climactic ending on the stage that was my childhood.

February 8, 2021

California

<A WILL>

Tonight, when I left the gala, my assistant told me that the cat from the gala was dead from anger. It was said for that perhaps I would be blamed.

The will from the cat was written as follows:

I was staring from afar at the artist, watching him eat the fish down to the bones. I thought that maybe he would leave a few pieces of fish meat between the crevices of the bones so that, when he leaves, I could sit down and put my mouth on it to get a few remaining smears or smudges. I could show off in front of my underlings. But I never could have imagined that not only was there no meat left; even the fishy smell was gone. To make matters worse, the second and third bones from the tail were stolen. Sigh. Before, when I was teaching Tiger, I made sure to keep a skill to myself, so the tiger never learned to climb trees, thus leaving our cat ancestors safe for ten generations. I lowered myself and from time to time collected some leftover pieces of meat and fish to sustain my cat family. Today, Tiger has kept to the original arrangement, but that human is no longer the same as before!

I can no longer sustain my offspring with my limited wisdom. How can I face the next generation of cats? Goodbye, my fellow cats!

Old cat
April 1, 2020
California Cat Studio

<CAT PERSONA>

Cat's temperament is lonely and cold, especially around the nose and eyes. I do not have to go forward or closer; I can feel the coldness from here. Perhaps it was the dark nose and sharp eyes that made the cat cold. They always squint and show a disdainful look at the world.

The cat's appearance tells the world that a lazy attitude may have been a better living method. Cats hide in the shadows all day, all year round, and don't move much in bright daylight. The cat's face is very similar and not very recognizable, just as when I look at people on the streets of New York and find that the people on the street are all the same. I care very little about cats, and cats care very little about me, which is fair. Cats can more easily than people achieve the status of Tao. Please don't think cats are brutal, cold, and cruel because they eat fish and catch mice. Eating fish and catching mice is their nature. This nature does not hinder their achievement of Tao.

I thought the cat owner must have a persona like a cat. It was later discovered that cat lovers are cat persona lovers. Cat lovers are both happily lonely and afraid of their loneliness. Perhaps this is the law of congregating. Cats have entirely comprehended the spirit of the human heart and mastered the law of survival: to be pampered, capture people's hearts, and balance between closeness and distance with humans. They are born with a pair of invisible cat paws to scratch the heart, which is why they are favored.

I have never seen cats be changeable or act by chance, and that cats don't often show the world their suffering and their hunger for life. It reminds me of the outliers of philosophers, artists, and writers who have always been indifferent and catlike. They always take the cat's eye, peer into the world, and see the world in cold and thin layers. The human way of life and emotional forms are approaching those of cats, and humans are beginning to care less about humans.

<MID-AUTUMN 2020>

Full moon shines upon the high mountains,

Darkened, the quiet Milky Way,

The cold stars lost in the blowing of the winds,

Honor or disgrace,

Follow their own path like wind and water flowing.

The youth leaves his nest,

Travels the unknown territory,

shoulders the burden of the world.

Tired, he understands the rationale of all,

Hometown across the ocean, stands long among Heaven
and the Earth,

Rest early tonight with no worry in the mind.

Gong

October 1, 2020

California

<COMPLETE>

Walk out the gate of Literature Conqueror,

Farewell to the songs of the Yellow River,

Break off the love to Pearl River,

Journey over the bridge across east and west.

Loyal since youth,

The burning passions of the young,

Practice of the morality and duty,

Nourish the seedling next.

Last lived on the golden peak,

Aerial view of the Milky Way torrents,

Heavenly dance in the lights of morning,

Growing old in the company of the moon and sun.

Gong

Yuebin Gong

November 20, 2020

California

<Joy for All>

Look upon the green hills.

Smell the yellow flowers,

Ah, see the blue sky!

Ah, see the clear river!

Sixty years of Springs and Falls.

Flowers sixteen years young.

This is California Sunshine.

This is my hometown.

A picnic on the grass, the sound of our laughter!

This is our song!

Hold a plate of dumplings,

Raise a cup of wine.

Our hearts full of feelings,

We slowly drink and sing.

Sixty years of nights and days,

But a sixteen-year-old heart.

This is my new hometown,

This is the love of family and friends.

We'll share our joy in this life!

This is inspired by our picnic lunch with friend Mike Lee on March 16, 2022.

<If Time Can Be Reversed>

Professor Wang pushed the centenarian in a wheelchair and played a skiing game on the pavement of the slopes, apparently with a boyish look. Professor Wang bowed his back like a tiger and pouted his big rear end; his feet in an outward position stepped alternately forward, hands pressing the balance handle, two lasering and confident eyes from behind his spectacle lenses gazing out like an arrow shot forward. The centenarian in the wheelchair giggled as the wind flashed forward. At that moment, Professor Wang decisively sent out the flying wheelchair and the centenarian with it.

"You are not afraid? Why are you so sure you are safe?" Bank manager Gong, walking next to him, looked at the centenarian lifted into the air along with the wheelchair and screamed. The wheelchair was running wild, and the centenarian in the wheelchair was laughing hysterically. Professor Wang, whose feet had been transformed into an inward posture, took a quick ride, watching the centenarian in the wheelchair that had passed through his rigorous mathematical calculations. The wind blew forward and spread backward the unstoppable laughter of the centenarian in the wheelchair. Professor Wang wiped the sweat from his forehead, stared at the speeding wheelchair ahead, and slowed it down. The wheelchair was preparing to fall back, as if the observer spacecraft had flown from Earth to Mars to complete a space exploration, automatically shifting gears, changing speeds, and slowly returning to Earth following its original orbit.

"Hey, hi! Are you not afraid? Don't you wonder why your wheelchair is sliding backward all the time?" the bank manager Gong, escorting them, nervously reminded the centenarian. Finally, the centenarian in the wheelchair smoothly slid to Professor Wang, with his body and arms formed in an arc for protection. The centenarian appeared shocked at first, then joyful, and then fell to laughter, like a baby being thrown in the air by her parent and back into the parent's arms. Professor Wang's face was reddened; sweat beads fell along his spiked shining hair. His appearance was that of a group of children used to the spirit and joy of the victory that came after challenging their parents. It seemed to tell people: time can be reversed.

Gong

November 22, 2020

California

<A LETTER TO MOTHER>

Dear Mother,

During the day, I'm so busy reading that I don't think of you much. But at night, I look again and again at the photos and videos my sister "Xiao Wei" shared in the family group chat. In the end, I always stop and linger at one video taken on October 2nd, where I see a familiar scene: my elderly 99 years old mother resembling an elementary school student, dutifully reading from the screen while weaving and bobbing her head back and forth. I glance at the time; it is 2:30 at night, but I can't bear to stop watching, can't bear to go to sleep. Every single little detail touches my heart and moves me deeply, I dare not miss a single thing.

Mother, the vision that filled my eyes was the sight of your silver hair, rhythmically dancing and swaying along, your strong hands, full of vitality, holding onto the table with full strength, and your feet stomping in time on the floor. I hear your oratorical voice while you recite,

"A good rain knows its seasons right:

In spring, it falls upon the ground.

With the wind, it sneaks into the night.

It moistens everything with no sound..." [1]

Looking at the sight of you wearing headphones and sitting in front of the screen monitor, I found that you have become the very picture of the best, most studious, and exemplary student sitting in the classroom, just like the students you taught in the past. As I think of the 24 hours a day diligent care and companionship from your daughter and your son-in law, all their toil and effort, at this moment, I want to write down the words, the heartfelt words your son has been unable to express, these words that have been blocked for the three years that you and I have been separated from each other by this span of ten thousand miles. At this age of 99 years old, that you can still preserve your eternal youthfulness, your passion, perseverance and willpower, and your heroic spirit is something that gives me incomparable pride and reverence. At the same time, I carry deeply within my bosom a wisp of unspeakable guilt and uneasiness.

Mother, whenever we have a video chat, the first sentence you always say to me after examining me for a while is "your hair and beard have completely turned white!" I understand the true meaning behind your words and the depth of your love for me. You are the person who know me best, you know best how I came from a malnourished and impoverished childhood, and how this life of mine was salvaged from the brink of death as a baby, bought back with a mere two dollars and fifty cents. How I crawled and struggled my way out of the impoverished and unfair environment of the rural countryside and made it to the city by revealing my talents and relying on my art studies. How I always held onto my original promises and intentions and stayed true to my dreams of becoming an artist, how I resolutely walked out of the Yellow River, bravely made my way in the world of the Pearl River (Guangdong), and ascended up in order to cross over the Pacific Ocean. Do you still remember? Because of my cleverness, my thoughtfulness, intelligence, and sensibleness, coupled with the fact that "poor families' children all grow up fast," all of these made up the virtues and conduct I carried myself with on my life path, and thus I am the only child out of your five children that have never suffered a beating from you. In a flash, I've become old too. I know you are the kind of mother that was as strict as a father and tender as a mother.

Mother, how deep is my love for you and our family, to never run out of things to say to you.

Mom, you and I are old now, and our hairs have turned white. Now we both have become muddled and confused, ignorant about the ways of the world. It seems that for both our generations, it is time for us to retire, to lay down the flag and silence the drums. Like the cicada's lifespan, we have already exhausted our spirits and our wisdom. But miraculously, we synchronized our rebirth, our change of fortunes as we both began our new lifestyles.

I believe it is because we possess in our blood the necessary Gong family spirit: a youthful, passionate, persevering, and bold heroic heart. As descendants of the Gong family's outstanding literary talents, we should follow their example and follow the changing of the times, by continuing our mission and open a new chapter in our lives. We practiced an old virtue: if you are diligent for a hundred years; the wise are tireless.

Mom, you have established a new motto for this new chapter of our lives. Your spirit, your mantra of "eat well, sleep well, read every day and you will be healthy," is the source of joy and happiness for our entire family. Just like this, I hope you keep happily reading every day, become the very image of your favorite kind of students, and always stay just as you have always been, upright, high-spirited, straight-backed. Go back to being the little girl you were ninety years ago, the little girl who fought and resisted against an entire family for her hunger and love of learning and her pursuit of knowledge.

Mom, it is now past 4 am. While my heart is currently overflowing with joy, love and warmth, I want to report to you my awakening, enlightenment and rebirth after that nightmare in 2018.

Mom, I am gratified and grateful as I look back at the past

60 years of my artistic life, which can be summarized by a trilogy of self-cultivation: to distinguish oneself through virtue, to distinguish oneself in business, and to distinguish oneself through one's writing."

I am grateful to you and to this era I was born in for raising me, a person who can, at all costs, reach to the very limits of my potential and capabilities, and exhaust all my aptitudes and skills. The me who exists right now, is currently only interested in studying and learning.

In the past 60 years, I have never experienced what it's like to genuinely pursue an education, and I've never understood the true meaning behind things like "interests" and "hobbies." Currently, all I want to do is to study, or to make up for my previous lack of education and knowledge.

Why have I made learning and studying my hobby? I think it's because the world has now become strange and unfamiliar to me, unapprehensible and unrecognizable, but my interests and hobbies are something I myself can attempt and manage, something that is self-sustaining, something that I can do without regard for fame and fortune, success and failure, gratitude and grievances, something that can be done with an indifferent attitude, and through this attitude of "it doesn't matter and it doesn't have worth," I can find its worth and value.

Mother, perhaps this is something I can still do; perhaps this is also a kind of gospel for our family.

Mother, I wish you a happy 99th birthday! May you always be happy and healthy!

Your son Little Bin

October 18, 2021

[1] A famous poem from Tang Dynasty Poet Du Fu

POSTFACE

<A Utopia for the Post-Trauma Artist>

The concept of this script came from my discussion of my uncle Gong's current state and his subliminal wishes for having an optimal life environment as a means of escape. Although the idea emerges out of my daily communication with Gong, it somehow informs a broader range of questions: How are we living? How do we want to live? Which parts of life are under our control? How do we deal with those beyond our control? Regardless, this piece takes shape as a manual-like narrative on concepts of space and life, where the ambiguous title, "A Utopia for the Post-Trauma Artist," requires additional elaboration to frame its preconditions.

"Utopia" might not be a precise definition for the concept, as the space here accommodates a personal realm instead of a society. Nevertheless, the term informs a state of isolation with illusory images of perfection that leave out any realistic conflict. These illusory images are created for the temporality of the artist's healing process, just like eggshells waiting for the chicks to break when they are ready. Instead of building a template of ideal life forms, this utopia intends to reflect on the artist's present life, to help articulate his desires and challenges in planning for his next journey. The appropriation of the term 'Utopia' may act as a wish that the artist would discover the perfect image for his future life while recovering from his trauma.

"Trauma" often points to a harsh strike to one's physical and psychological states with its impact persisting in the aftermath of the event. In the case of Gong, however, the trauma transcends the impact scope of the strike itself and has been shifting toward a sense of conflict between the artist's present life and his past glory. He is traumatized not only by the overwhelming shadows of his previous achievements that dwarf his weak present but also through the romanticized images of old days that trigger his endless doubts about the changing world. Unless he can truly understand and accept his present life, the trauma will persist and make his every moment vulnerable to self-abasement.

"Artist" indicates not only Gong's career in art production but also the expected state of life that the utopia would reinvent for him: He has to build an artistic perspective to see himself and the surrounding world when fighting against his trauma. An artistic mindset was especially important after he stepped down from the role of active social production that once filled his understanding of life. The new art he has to create is no longer defined by its media impact or commercial value, but by the enjoyment of the creator himself. It can be projects of literary and visual dialogues, delicate dishes prepared for a fine glass of wine, or even the daily observation of sunglows above the bay. The essence here is to draw the artist's full dedication, leaving no chance for the trauma to act on his life.

1. The utopia sits on a mountain that oversees the bay. The sense of distance flattens the city into a background image at the horizon, while the inconvenience of the height reduces the adjacent town into a few retail shops and marketplaces that link to the utopia only on an occasional basis. The position naturally rejects a major part of the mundane life that would have bothered the artist, leaving only a small portion to be dissolved within the utopia.

2. Waking up among songbirds and streaming water, the artist starts his day with morning exercise in the backyard. Unlike any routine moves guided by a designed track, the dynamic gestures of his body incarnate dialogues with everything that is showered under sunlight: the air, the birdsongs, the streams, the plants, and

even the skyline of the rising city across the bay. All these moments collectively assemble an ephemeral artwork that only exists for the morning.

3. After finishing his last move, the artist turns to the kitchen while the mundane elements are popping up in the yard: pool cleaning, garden maintaining, warehouse remodeling, among an infinite list. However, the glass door filters all these matters out of the artist's vision, framing his passions on to his next project: the art of making a perfect breakfast. Although the project only spans less than ten minutes, the artist considers it a significant challenge in his career, as it has to satisfy his increasingly fastidious taste. When the project comes out hot from the pan, the dining table is suddenly filled with guests who cheer for their ability to share the enjoyment of this masterpiece. The artist stages the plates in the bay view, evaluating them visually and by taste while sharing his inspirations and workflows with his guests. Judging by everyone's mouth-filled smiles, the artist knows that today's creation has been a huge success!

4. Walking out of the kitchen, the artist finds his ongoing art project reemerging in the studio area, on the same spot where it vanished the last evening. It indicates that the utopia has approved him to work at his full load. This extraordinary

passion for hard work has been used to support the artist's career, leading him to great accomplishment, fame, and wealth. In the utopia, however, the chasing of socially defined success is removed from the artist's instinct alongside his past glory. He has to rediscover his great passion to power up his chasing an internal art that can dissolve his trauma. Dazzling in the brainstorm and sprinkling with sweat, the artist pictures the contours of an emerging masterpiece. Meanwhile, the studio area is filled with numerous figures, whose faces and voices vaguely resemble the acquaintances from the artist's past journeys around the world. They walk around the project, helping the artist to position his progress through comments of admiration and confusion, or harsh critiques. In dialogues of explanation, discussion, and debate, the artist finds himself closer to his once-familiar sense of confidence, which brings him one step closer to the day of leaving the utopia.

5. Suddenly, the great project vanishes from the studio area while the charming aroma of food spreads from the dining room. The utopia is sending a signal that the artist has been more than overworked: he is not allowed to work even on smaller projects such as lunch making! After finishing the delicious food prepared by the utopia, the artist sits on his favorite beach chair,

looking at the distant mountains that are lifted by fogs over the bay and tracing the airplanes that rise from the other side of the mountains. While recovering with his creative passion, he somehow links this distant landscape to the philosophical pieces that he did not comprehend when reading them days ago. As his thoughts evolve, his friends, colleagues, and family members pop up one after another, forming an instant salon that points to the spectacle of the bay. The artist sits among them with eyes half closed, shifting his thoughts between the various points of the discussion and occasionally bringing new questions to the salon. When the salon comes to an end and the participants vanish in succession, the artist looks back at the studio area and finds it still empty. " So, I am still not capable of continuing working on my big project, right? But at least let me write something on this fantastic salon," he mutters, sits back, and find his notebook waiting on the side table alongside his reading glasses and a fine cup of tea.

6. As the artist switches his eyes between the notebook and the bay, the sun moves toward the city at horizon, and the light gradually goes faint. The artist takes off his glasses and decides to take a walk that can help him digest his thoughts. When walking across the yard that has been neatly cleaned by the utopia, he notices today's

great progress on the warehouse remodeling work. He is satisfied with the overview of the progress but does not intend to take a closer look. The utopia has been keeping him distant from such works that would otherwise entangle his mind in endless, noncreative tasks. The only thing he knows is that the warehouse will eventually transform into a teahouse, upon his wish to have a better view at teatime.

7. The artist walks across the mountain as the night falls. The golden sun sinks at the horizon; the descending blueness pushes the remaining gold down to the other side of distant mountains. While the sky blends into the same color, the earth lights up with countless sparkles from thousands of homes. This precious art of sky and ground offers enormous inspiration to the artist's mind. After returning to the utopia, he applies his instant ideas into his big project, which has reappeared just in time. In addition, the inspiration from this walk is embodied in his creation of tonight's dinner.

8. Nevertheless, the utopia does not grant much working time to the artist due to the limitation of his current physical capacity. As soon as the last touch of blueness turns into pure black, his big project vanishes again alongside the lighting of the studio area. Although the artist is pissed off for a moment by this forced withdrawal from

overexcitement, his attention quickly turns toward the fireplace, where a whisky is waiting for him. As he sits in front of the crackling fire, the wall turns into a gigantic screen, playing the title of tonight's selected film. The artist finally accepts the fact that he will not be able to see his project again before the next morning. He takes a sip from the glass, leaving his creative ideas behind and enjoying the movie night.

Haoyu, nephew of the author

May 1, 2021

California

GRATITUDE

Walk another sixty years along the vision and warmth of the equator!

Gratitude: sixty years of bathing under the light of the South Pole.

Gratitude: the nightmare of 2018 following the cold of the North Pole.

Gratitude: the Yellow River, Pearl River, and Pacific Ocean making up the spring of "Reincarnation."

Gratitude: Long-lasting blood of the family nourishing the power of the magnetic field.

*** *** ***

Great-Grandfather: Gong Yuzhu (1867–1919), courtesy name DiTang, Juren from late Qing Dynasty, Emperor GuangXu gifted him three plaques: "Conqueror of the Classics," "Virtue Across All," " Host of Benevolence,"

<恩同罔积>; Henan province, Luoyang City, Yianshi District, Koudian Town, Gongjiayao Village.

Grandfather: Li Hengyue (1896–1942), courtesy name JingBai, Family Trade Name: Xi Taiheng; a gentry. Henan Province, Luoyang City, Yianshi District, Koudian Town, Liuli Village.

Father: Gong Shangzhi (1921–1986), teacher.

Mother: Li Yunsheng (1923), teacher; City of Yianshi government granted two plaques to her: "Family of Teachers," "Ten Best Mother." In 2019, she was awarded National Medal during National Day celebration.

Gong Yuebin, Chinese America artist. Born in 1960. Studied in Luo Yang Normal University and Guangzhou Academy of Fine Art. Immigrated to America in 2003. Artworks were exhibited and collected in California State University, Sacramento, Crocker Art Museum, and France. In 2012, he received recognition from Congressman and state Senator. For his visual artwork, please check his website at: www.gongyuebin.com

Gong

November 22, 2020

California

125

YUEBIN GONG

PART II

IN CHINESE

十六岁六十

作者：宫跃斌

编辑：宫工作室 /Jessica Hatch

翻译：宫田/黄恺琳

设计：王皓宇/Pressbook

编审：黄嫩环

出版：IngramSpark

印刷：IngramSpark

目录

《序》

和小舅同住在湾区躲避疫情的这半年里，我们二人一直活在日常之外：我在读写中探索无法抵达的城市，小舅则在文学哲学巨著中重新解读自己过去的六十年。我们每日各自浸泡在自己的世界中，只有在阳光下吃早餐或是在炉火旁小酌时才会用时事话题做引子，尝试着阐述、理解、和解构对方的世界。在日复一日的碎片式交流中，我逐渐拼接出这本书的轮廓，但却难以构建出为书作序所需的要素：这本书讲述了一个怎样的故事？它在对谁讲述？它想要传达怎样的观点？小舅带着对我们思维差异性的期待邀请我作序，但我认为与其用自己的思维和书稿搏斗，不妨暂且抛开书中内容，从我的视角重建一幅《十六岁六十》的样貌。相比起面向读者的序言，我下面的文字更像是面向小舅下一个六十年寄出的前言，也希望藉此为读者提供另一个理解本书的维度。

在我的成长过程中，小舅扮演的角色一直都是 "遥远的强大人影"。无论是家人口中传奇的南下创业故事，从广州延伸到美国的庞大家业，还是偶尔到访加州与他短暂的交流，**带给**我的都是一个目光**远**大意气风发的**伟**岸形象。对于**习惯**扮演**隐**形边**缘**角色的我来**说**，这种人格形象仅仅是一个**遥**不可及的影子。而父母**则**在我画画的**爱**好中找到了和小舅的共通点**来**激励我向这个强大人影学**习**。从学画画到赴美留学，小舅的人影一直引**导**着我在成长岔路口做出的决定。然而直到我搬**来**加州和小舅共同生活，才发**现**他本人其实也是在这个强大人影的操控下前**进**。在阳光下和炉火边的对**谈**中，我可以看到他六十年间如何在社会的泥沼中一步步构建出这个无**坚**不摧的人影，如何在它的**驱**动下不断前**进**，又在经历了突发的磨**难**后在它面前**产**生恐惧，因**为**自己如今不符合它的期望而彷徨无措。小舅**说**自己前六十年一直在把周遭世界当作一面用来修正和完善自己人格的**镜**子。如果是这面**镜**子塑造了我所见的这个强大人影，那么把**镜**中**陆续**加入的打拼，前**进**，**伤**害，文化冲**击**等元素逐一剥除后，能看到他的本源**吗**？

在这半年里，我和小舅的大多对**谈**都是在**尝试**共同**寻**找强大人影**笼**罩下真实的他。我从社会**层**面入手解剖他几十年来人影形成的过程，而小舅从哲学角度出发**寻**找自己人格的根基。在这个过程中，那个熟悉的人影突然变成了他思**维**中的**拦**路虎，用过去六十年沉浮的经验和功名**垄**断了对他自己内心和周遭世界的解**释权**，阻碍了他的**进**一步探索。而如今退出事业奋斗前**线**的小舅也失去了用他的**镜**子**进**一步改造这个人影的能力。即使是他**恶**补的文学哲学著作和与我共同梳理的社会知**识**，在冲撞这个人影后也只能留下可以**为**它所用的部分。**为**了避开这个人影，我**们**把聚焦点逐步定格在小舅的十六**岁**：一个已经**认识**到世界的黑暗面却还没有开始与之正面博弈的年**龄**。在特殊年代暗无天日的社会环境下，十六**岁**是小舅最后一段可以自由探索世界的时光，也是他在强大人影形成之前最后一个塑造自我的机会。彼时他眼中的世界可以是院子里的桃树，也可以是速写本上的戏台，它们既代表不了那个时代的全貌，也不会帮助他走出黑暗去往远方，但它们体现着少年面对至暗时最纯粹的自我表达。在小舅碎片化的讲述中，我可以看到一个十六岁的人格渐渐从六十岁的强大人影中破茧而出。

我并不认为这本书能够纪实复刻小舅十六岁时所处的社会，抑或是他完整的内心世界。作为一个在社会之镜中不断重塑自己，驾驭着强大人影又被人影裹挟的人，小舅渴望在写作中找回的或许只是被人影遮蔽的那一小部分十六岁。在六十岁的节点上，小舅提出了下一个阶段多听少做的人生宣言，这不仅意味着他要褪去社会沉浮中的阴影，重拾对这个世界光明一面的好奇心，还意味着他要与自己长期塑造的强大人影宣战。在这场可能并不容易的战争中，小舅需要的不是缅怀或重新种出少年的十六棵桃树，而是找回和桃树对话的精神去探索属于六十岁的那片竹林，对这种精神的追寻也构成了我对这本书最大的期待。我衷心希望他能在写作中找到下一段人生所需的灵感和力量，信心十足地对那个熟悉的人影说：谢谢你六十年的支持，如今我要开始亲自探索这个世界啦！

作者的外甥

王皓宇

01/01/2021 于加州

《1960》

———❧———

我出生于1960年，一个黄河边上的小村庄。生时逢**艰**，**艰**时逢生，我像只在干**瘪**的土地上硬**挤**出来的崽子。人们常**骂**我"狗崽子"，皆因我的家世和境遇。这时令，这名号，我不曾在意过。我以**为**动**荡**和摇晃，是西风不淑的**缘**故。

老天似乎也不愿过多地着墨于这片生我育我的土地，只是**轻**描淡写的**给**了两笔。一笔**蓝**，一笔黄，这便是我的天地了。那黄河边上稀稀疏疏、**隐隐约约**的人间呢，不过是老天不小心**遗**落的墨点，零零落落的。

烈日把大地烤晒到皮开肉裂，裂得炸开，裂出了深深浅浅的**皱纹**和沟壑，没有了血脉。地表像被刀刻出的一块又一块的脆**饼**，**摊**在天空之下。

西风一冷，日子也冷。那抹**蓝**，那抹黄，经西风吹旧，经日晒雨淋，**鲜**色褪去，成了灰褐，落上了雪。

《宫家窑》

风，呼呼地吹，吹什么呢？还有什么可吹的呢？越吹越荒凉。停止吧，凄厉的风。风，从西边来，要到西边去，把什么都吹没了。"古道西风瘦马"的悲凉流转到了今天。有西风的地方，人残马瘦。这里的土地像是被风席卷了很久很久，吹走了一层又一层，从西边吹到了更远的西边，只剩下瘦瘦的一层薄皮，什么都长不出来。

我们家姓宫。这里的人都姓宫，住在宫家窑。是黄河边上伊洛南岸的一个小村庄，大约有一百来人。说起这个姓氏，是极其少有的。听说，很久以前，皇帝让一些宫人们出了宫，赐给他们这个姓氏。姓宫的人在此生根发芽，烧起了窑，就叫"宫家窑"。烧窑倒是个过活的好法子，这里除了烧窑，也想不出什么好法子过活。远远看去，每家每户的房子都是黄土色的，俨如窑一般。人们从窑洞里进进出出，从窑里出来，还要回到窑里去，整个人都是灰头土脸的。

我的直觉告诉我，这片土地的历史已经很久远了，久远到让人遗忘了，久远到失去了自己的身份。这片土地上，埋藏了许多过去所不为人知的秘密。在这份贫瘠当中，隐藏着华夏古都的繁华盛世。只是人们都在忙于生死，无暇顾及这份神秘。

宫家的先祖未曾离开过这里吗？他们为何不到别处生存？他们没有走出过这片荒凉吗？我想找回这块土地的身份。幻想的种种，疑惑的种种，想着，想着，便睡着了。在梦中，一群游牧，浩浩荡荡，马肥人壮，从黄河那头慢慢地迁移过来。他们在此栖息扎营，生儿育女，开枝散叶。后来，繁华消散，人仰马翻。一切，都让风刮走了。如今，留守在这里的人们如同出土文物一般，残败不堪。

当太阳升起的时候，一片光辉覆盖大地，即便是块贫瘠的土地，我仍能感受到上帝的仁爱。当太阳落下的时分，又会黯淡下来，发出几声叹息。太阳与月亮，对这块土地照射出虔敬的光。我依然有许多愿望。

我渴望读书，渴望上进。我喜欢奔跑在山梁上听风。当我奔跑在高高的山梁上时，我告诉自己，脚步快一点，再快一点。风从耳朵里窜进来，似乎，真能听出个什么来。东风吹绿，南风吹暖，北风吹雪，西风吹荒，各风吹着各风的故事。

童年做着童年的梦，顾不得太多。哪个孩子不天真？哪个孩子不爱做梦？可我的童年，给我讲故事的人太少了。

《大风吹》

风一来，如**恶**人**进**村，翻天掀地的，经过蛮横的**扫荡**，村里像被洗劫了一样，**连**沙都留不住。

风一来，整个村子屏息了**起来**，听风的嚎叫。地上的吹上了天，天上的吹下了地。天，成了地；地，成了天。人**们**倒着走，眼睛要倒着看。人**们**低着头，像是风把他**们**的脖子吹断了，抬不起头。风，长了**恶**人的嘴**脸**，无所不能，还能拐着弯，追着人。风一来，寸步**难**行，躲也躲不掉。人若走在路上，要么把人吹到左边，要么把人吹到右边，一条路，两边倒。人在风中，站**起来**，吹倒，站**起来**，吹倒，不如就地躺下，躺下也不行，会被风送去天边的。

风，把人吹出了**许**多"病"。有的人禁不起风，被风一吹，**连**个人影都没了。有的人，被风一吹，得了"风病"，倒地不起。有的人，被风一吹，得了狂**热**病，着了魔。父亲被风一吹，得了痴呆症，**终**日默默不**语**，低着头，忽笑忽哭。有的人家，被吹得家破人亡。母亲也被吹倒过，幸好，站了**起来**。她**缠**过足，比三寸金**莲**长一点点。风一来，她就咬着牙，**紧紧**地抓着厚实的地，比风还要倔强，任它如何吹。风见她如此，只好灰溜溜地走了。我时常见她，在大风天里，一步一步地走，走得很低很低，抵着风。这里的人，要么低着头，要么弯着腰。

风，是一条**线**，串着过去、**现**在和未来，串着天、地、人。风一抽身，过去、**现**在、未来断了，散落了一地，成了故事。风一来，又把故事串成了篇。有时候，风自己翻着篇，**说**着故事，我且听且看。宫家窑，像个被风吹倒的大罐子，碎成石**砾**、瓦片，四处散落。

有时候，风把太阳吹得灰头土**脸**的，失去了**鲜**丽的光；有时候，风把云都吹散了。那云本是一团团的，厚厚的，风把云吹成了**一丝丝**，**一缕缕**，薄薄的，在天空中散开。有的人，被风吹得没有了棱角，**圆圆**滚滚的；有的人，却被风吹出了棱角，刀一样的**锋**利。每每，我看到一副**恶嘴脸**，我想，大约是被西风吹歪的。

《家》

黄昏的光越来越少，**渐渐**的，**连**最后一**丝**的光**线**都被收走了。天和地变得**浑浊**起来，暗多，明少。天幕仍是**蓝**，是靛**蓝**加了一滴墨汁勾兑出来的深**蓝**。**蓝**出了一种高度和深意，**蓝**出了天空中最亮的星。屋**顶**上老**树**的**树**杈落尽了叶子，如枯**涩**的鬼手一般魅惑，在深**蓝**之中无序地伸**张**，**说**不出的**诡**异。我家的灯还没有亮起来，**爷爷**家的灯已经亮了起来。

昏黄的灯，是每家每户门前的星。我把凳子搬到可以照到光**线**的地方，开始写起了作业。

爷爷喊我——"尖儿"。"尖儿"是我的小名。有时候他**们**喊我"三尖子"。我上头有两个哥哥，我排在兄弟中最末。我"嗯"了一下，**连**头都不抬一下。

村里人常叫我"反革命的狗崽子"，我亦**习惯**了。我从不反抗，也很少答理，我总是小心翼翼的，**习惯**低头走路，**说话结结**巴巴的。我和我**爷爷**本不大亲**热**，自然**习惯**了不吱声。

爷爷见我不大待见他，便火起来了。"兔崽子，没大没小。**爷爷**也不叫了。你爸傻了，你也呆了。"他**骂**了一会儿，**觉得骂**的始**终**是自己的骨肉，**骂**自己似的。

那天，我一**进**门，看见二哥在客**厅**里跪着。我**问**他："你怎么在地上跪着？"，"**让**他自己**说**！"母亲凌厉的声色，着实把我吓了一跳。二哥低着头，一**脸**沮**丧**，嘟嘟囔囔，支支吾吾的。看来，二哥又**闯祸**了。大哥、大姐准备升高中，都懂事了；我还小，开始懂事，自然不会**闯祸**；而二哥，正处于一个不大不小**闯祸**的年**龄**，隔三差五得母亲的**训**。在小事上，我比他聪明；但是，他**读书**比我好。我懂得眼色，懂得如何**讨**好人。二哥心性憨厚，心思总是粗糙**许**多。我的懂，是退怯，是安静，是对父母的周全。原来，家里的**鸡**死了，母亲把它**给**煮了，把**鸡**腿分出来，想**给**村长送过去当作"人情"，恳求村长，看看能否在村里开办一个学前教育班，目的是**为**了村里未**满**上学年**龄**的孩子能够接受学前教育。母亲正要准备拿这只**鸡**腿去**说**事，**结**果，二哥一看厨房有煮熟的**鸡**腿，**问**也不**问**就在**鸡**腿上偷啃了一口。也怪不得他，那时候实在都**饿**得慌，肉更是**难**得一见的稀奇。

听母亲**说**，这个方案的提**议**出于公，也出于私。母亲在外村教**书**，离家**约**有几里地。平日，上**课教书**走不开，只能周末回家。我又未够**岁**数上一年**级**。父亲因被划成右派被迫下放劳动在生**产队**看猪，他胆小又怕事，经不起政治上的打**击**，精神失常整天唯唯**诺诺**的。**妈让**他帮忙照看我，他总是**连**忙摇头**说**："别，别，别，我不行"。母亲心疼同**龄**的学生整日像野孩子放任自流，更放心不下我无人照看。母亲的提**议终**于得到了**乡**里的重视与落实，像我这样的孩子**们终**于在学前有了呵护。

我的母亲叫李芸生，出生于1923年，**毕**业于省立洛阳女子中学。她是洛阳刘李村里一个大户人家的小姐，她的父**辈们**是方**圆**百里的**乡绅贵**族。因**为**遭到同行的嫉妒与暗算，她的父亲在她十五**岁**的时候被害身亡。母亲一出生就患了眼疾，**终**身落下了只有一只视力的眼睛。虽出身在封建时代里的一个地主家庭，她并不屑于荣华富**贵**、胭脂水粉，却十分渴慕**读书**求**识**。家中的长**辈**不同意她上学，她就**绝食抗议**，**终**成**为**那个年代少有的知**识**女性。

我的父亲宫尚志，出生于1920年，**毕**业于延安**鲁**迅师范学院。1938年由地下革命党**带领**到延安**读书**参加革命，曾就**职**于延庆教委。后回到洛阳与我母亲**结**婚，他**们**一同在城里教**书**。1959年，双双被打成右派，下放到农村改造。

父亲自从政治上受到打**击**后，一直处于似醒非醒、恍恍惚惚、担惊受怕的状**态**。前几年是自言自**语**，不时地笑，这几年**话**更少了，只是抽烟。常常，母亲在洗衣服，父亲在门口抽烟。母亲劝道："别抽烟了吧，身体都抽坏了"，父亲**说**："我什么都没了，唯独这口烟了，烟亡人亡。"，母亲听后便**说**："那就少抽一些吧"。 父亲的命苦，要是能哭出来，大概也就能好起来了。

母亲后来恢复了公**职**，在当地当起了**乡**村教师，每个周末才能回家一天。我最熟悉的母亲回来的画面：母亲总是**带**着匆匆的步子从前院走到后院，**刚进**后院的门，就开始解扣子，脱大衣，挽袖子，**进**厨房，里里外外地忙乎着，她总能找出各种"活"一刻不停的干。母亲在，这个家才有了生气。她虽只有一只眼睛的视力，但对生活从来是不模糊的；虽是小脚，但从来没有摔倒过。对待这个家，她总是有办法。

"李老师，对不起啊，能不能借点面？家里那几个崽子正长身体，吃得过头了。队里发粮了，我还你。"隔壁的邻居站在门口对母亲说。母亲没有丝毫的为难，进厨房，端了一碗面给她。她谢了一声，走了。母亲对乡邻，总是很慷慨。在我的记忆中，家里再困难，从未问过别人家借一粒粮食。这倒不是面子的事，而是心态。母亲从不纵容我们，宁愿吃差一点，却能吃得长远。她不愿意为饱一、两顿口腹之欲，后面的日子青黄不接。每逢过节，各家的小孩子总爱聚在一块，把好吃的端出来炫耀；而我，从不敢端着碗出去，因为我的碗里太寒酸了。父亲总说："你妈做的饭总是不僧不俗，米里掺沙"。但凡父亲能说句清楚的话，我都是高兴的。

每当队里分配粮食，我们家的面袋总是比别人家的小很多。我问母亲，为何家里人口多，分配的却是最少的。母亲告诉我，多了，扛不动。后来，才知道，母亲在学校教书，领工资，无工分。这是队里给我家的定额分配，别人家的不仅有定额分配的，还有工分所得的，自然比我们家多了。母亲时常把白面与红薯面和在一起。表皮是薄薄的一层白面，里面是厚实的黑的红薯面。只在过年的时候才能吃到纯白面的馒头。热热的，沉沉的，绵绵的，像个雪球，和那云一样白净，听说，牛奶也是这样的白，但从未喝过。

我们家在村里显得格格不入。村里人说我们——讲究。至于如何讲究，我也不明白。我们不讲脏话，也不会骂人，被骂了也不反抗。教书的教书，读书的读书。一家子很安静。每到了晚饭过后，母亲为了省油，只在堂屋的饭桌上点起一盏灯，大伙围着灯，对着书，拿着笔，各做各事。屋里只有翻书和写字的声音。我家有兄弟姐妹五个，却只有一两**盏**灯。人多，灯少。灯在哪里亮着，人就往哪里呆着。总之，人随灯走。在那个时候，不**讲**究的人比**讲**究的人过的富裕。知**识**是体面，生活是窘迫。

有一回，母亲去外婆家取粮食。听**说**是舅**妈**偷偷**瞒**着表哥对我**们**家的接济。母亲去了快两个小时还不见踪影，眼看天快黑了，大家都在屋里等着，担心了起来。大哥提**议**大家出动，一起拉车去接母亲。我**们**在下坡的路上，**远远**看着一个人坐在地上哭泣，她望着天空，又好像望着**远**处的山。一种无望和**绝望**。是母亲！她旁边放着两袋粮食。她想到自己过去曾是**贵**族家中的掌上明珠，因**为**自己的倔强，不甘，和时令荒芜，落得今天这般田地，叫天天不**应**，叫地地不灵，悲从中来，便哭了起来。我甚少见母亲落泪。

大伙儿合力推拉着，**继续**上路。大哥力气大，在前面拉着，其余就都在后面推着。我跟着跑着，跑不动了，哭了起来。母亲把我抱上车。我坐上了推车，高高在上，**觉**得好玩，高兴地笑了起来。大哥一见我**乐**呵，便用手掌拍了一下我**脑**壳，我**顿**时不敢出声，嘟着嘴，但心里还是偷着**乐**。到了上坡处，大家也都快没了力气，**许**是天黑，路也模糊了，**结**果车一歪翻了，粮食撒了**许**多，我也从车上掉下来，母亲一把抓住我，我差点掉**进**旁边的一口井里，人就在井口边上了。母亲**紧紧**地拽着我。好不容易快到了，粮食又撒了一地。悲又重来，**我们**又哭了**一场**。

回到家中，父亲点着了灯等**我们**。人在，灯亮。灯，原是**一盏**火，被罩住，就成了灯。家，原来是一个屋子，人聚在一起，就成了家。

《放学》

"狗崽子，放学啦？长大了可和你爸一样看猪？你可看不了猪　，猪可比你跑得快多了。"几个乡邻坐在石板凳上抽着烟，闲聊着。每次见到我，他们总要嬉笑我一番。我背着书包，不吭一声，只往家里冲。

这些人，是不得消闲的。在地里放不下锄头，在命运里放不下铜臭。我知道，他们放不下穷。

我家是被这些人常议论的，"这家子人口多，干活少，家里有过举人又如何？吃了几代了？还不是照样败下来了。富不过三代呀。宫举人到现在他们，刚好三代"。

我在村里都是躲躲闪闪的，因为他们的眼光，也因为他们的闲言碎语。在我读小学三年级的时候，母亲又被派回到宫家窑小学教书。这样一来，我便与母亲一同进出，我比之前走得松爽了许多。

在那些年，每家每户都养着两、三头猪。每天，猪都要去生产队的猪圈里"集合"，目的是为了把猪聚集起来产粪、圈肥。学校的隔壁就是猪圈。一到中午，铃声一响，人放学，猪也"放学"。学生们和猪一涌而出。人头，猪头，一头头。人，**竖**着走，猪，横着走。学生一看这么多猪，**觉**得好玩，便赶着，追着，吓着，笑着。猪经不起**闹**，一头猪跑了，大家都惊慌失措地跑起来了，不管不**顾**，你推我拱。人和猪相撞；人和人相撞；猪和猪相撞；猪和人相撞。人追着猪跑，人笑着，猪叫着。猪跟着猪跑，喘着气。

一头头猪，撅着屁股，卷着尾巴，四条雪白的腿撑着白粉的身子，一跑起**来**，肚子上挂着肉，晃**荡**晃**荡**的。短拙的猪腿由粗到**细**，由**细**到尖，最后，踮着尖蹄子抵在地，看起来就像是一个穿着高跟鞋的胖女人，有些优雅，有些吃力，**一颠一颠**的。那猪蹄子又短又粗，虽短小，却也精悍，往前奔的时候，猪蹄子踏着土地，**扬**起了尘土，头**顶**着两把扇子似的耳朵，在风中**显**得迷乱。跑着跑着，有些慌，失了方寸，迷了方向，不知怎地跑到别人家，一看不是自家，**一脸**茫然，不道别一声，只从喉**咙**和鼻子里面"哼哼"两声，**闷闷**的，掉头就走。

它**们**，总归不会将**错**就**错**，总归是要回到自己的家。

《看戏》

上次看戏是什么时候，**记**不清了。这些天，有戏班子**来**村里唱戏，台下摆着一排排板凳，老老实实地等待**开场**。

那戏台搭出了一个光景，一**丛红**黄**蓝绿**的光景。赤荒之中一点**红**，一点黄，一点**绿**，对于孩子**来说**都是隆重的。荒村的**颜**色实在苦，且寡淡。就单单这点明亮，**让**人一下子从苦**涩**的滋味中逃离出来。那戏子的长衣和胡子，还有五花八门的妆容在**脸**上**绽**放，不知道是哭还是笑。喜的当悲唱，悲的当喜唱，戏如人生，永**远**看不清当中的真相。台下的人不管戏子是哭，是笑，是悲，是喜，只管鼓掌叫好。这就是看戏。

我坐在台下的一个角落，形单影只的，**远远**地看着一些与我年**龄**相仿的的孩子在戏台上笑着，**闹**着，跑着，追打着。我**认**得他**们**，都是大**队**干部的孩子。他**们**穿得光**鲜**，伶伶俐俐的。他**们**的笑**闹**在**释**放，没有阻挡的**释**放，整个戏台都是他**们**的欢声笑**语**，**让**人看着羡慕。仿佛，只有他**们**才是新出生的太阳。我心生落寞，我渴望上台，但我明白，我是没有上台**资**格的孩子。我心生第一个梦想，梦想成**为**大**队**支**书**的儿子。

我掏出藏在我棉袄里的速写本，在台下起**劲**的画起我看到的。我看着那戏台，那戏台也看着我。不料，大**队**民兵**营**长走到我跟前，来者不善的样子，好像我犯了什么罪似的。我抬起头看他，当时，心有点慌。他看着我，不**语**，又低头看我的画本，我不想**让**他看，便用手挡着，他一把**抢**过去，翻着，看着，冷笑的**讥讽**："你画画？画的什么？你还有**资**格画画？撒泡尿照照**镜**子，你一个反革命狗崽子还有**资**格画画？！" 说完，把我的画本撕碎摔在地上，指着我，一边走，一边嘟嘟嚷嚷、**骂骂**咧咧地离去。我**捡**起碎在地上的画本，不生气，**觉**得有些委屈和冷慌。想回家，但是戏正要开演。回家还是看戏？算了，回家吧。

当时，我还不懂戏，更没有上台的机会，却莫名遭受了一**场恶**剧，心中的戏台塌了。没想到，台下比台上的戏更滑稽，更荒**诞**。那**恶人恶**剧，自然是不会上戏台的，上戏台的当然都是风光的。那**阔**大的幕布呈**现**着庄**严**之气，**直摄**人心，一副义正言辞，好像要告**诉人们**什么。

往后，每到看戏时，这幕又上心头，莫名地**觉**得，戏没有了意思。

《红薯》

每到**红薯**收获的季**节**，家家户户的地里都躺着一根根**刚**出土的**红薯**，**带**着薯藤，如同**刚**从大地中脱胎，还没来得及剪断**脐带**的**婴**儿。身上沾着泥，**带**着新**鲜**的泥味，**连**根拔起后，躺在地上歇着气。就这样从地里出生了，一副茫然未知的模样，不知何去何从。

煮**红薯**，蒸**红薯**，烤**红薯**，**红薯**干，**红薯**粉，**红薯**面，**红薯汤**……天天吃，年年吃，一吃就是十八年。日子不停，**红薯**不停。**红薯进**入嘴巴里，**绵绵**的，还粘着舌头，沾滞在喉**咙**上。不剥皮的样子挺傻的，剥了皮的样子也傻。在大冷天里吃**红薯**，**红薯**冒着气，我的嘴巴哈着气，一口一口地吃，心平气和地吃，**红薯**不能吃快了，不然，会**烫**了**肠**肚堵了气血。

从我出生到十八**岁**，**红薯**，是我童年唯一的食物，我是吃**红薯**长大的孩子。舌头除了咸和甜，只**认**得出一种味道–**红薯**味。而至于其他味道，在那时候是没有机会**尝**到的。一根根的**红薯**，在家的地窖里屯着，如山一般的堆**积**，好像告**诉**我，这日子将被**红薯**所埋葬。要是这**红薯**变成一堆白面那多好呀？

每天走出校门，学生们和猪们总是一场交战，大多都是饿了。人饿了，猪也饿了，各自回家寻吃的，吃着相同的红薯，嚼出不同的味道，全村长空弥漫着那熟悉得不能再熟悉的红薯味。

"妈妈"，我边脱书包，边喊着母亲。"妈，今天吃什么？"，即便我知道是红薯，却还是忍不住问，盼望着揭开锅盖能有一次惊喜。"锅里有红薯，趁热吃吧！"。那甜熟的热气随盖而出，扑鼻而来。熟透的红薯在锅里躺着，皮开肉绽，不知是哭还是笑，短短的，拙拙的，有的裂开了皮，露出了里面黄黄的肉。贴锅的红薯，大约快被烧焦了，锅底一层黑黑的红薯糖汁。我挑了一根，一块薯皮贴着锅，不愿出来，我用舌头舔舔沾在那红薯身上的糖汁，甜甜的。红薯是甜软的，可人饿的时候，嘴巴却渴望着咸味。

"妈，咸菜呢？"，"没了，过几天吧。你哥把最后一点吃完了。"红薯被剥开，看着无味，吃着也无味，但还是要吃，不吃怎么办呢？最后，我把它们剥了皮，掰开一块块，放在碗里用筷子挑碎，挑烂，加了盐，看了妈一眼，又加了点油，成了红薯泥，黄黄的，蓉蓉的。有了油和盐，吃着是不一样了，想着要是加上些许葱蒜，那就成了我家后院小土坡上的桃花园啦。

我感觉还不过瘾，吃完红薯泥，大约饱了六分。我看看灶炉下面还有火，便把两根生的红薯扔了进去，用炭火把它们埋起来。约十多分钟，香气就会冒出来。黑乎乎的，像碳一样黑，皮上冒着烟，两头尖还点着火星子。把烤好的红薯剥开两瓣，烫手！皮焦肉嫩。呵！真甜。

看看糖罐里还有糖没。打开，只剩下空罐子。用力摇一摇，摇出了一些糖渣子。找来勺子，把糖罐边上的糖渣子用勺子一刮，刮出了半勺子。用拇指和食指捻住白糖，搓开，分别撒在烤好的**红**薯上。白糖如雪降落。啊！我的世界下雪了！一块**红**薯有了白雪的覆盖，精致了**许**多。**许**多年后成了甜的**记忆**。

红薯，会**让**人吃出麻木。舌头是麻木的，眼睛是麻木的，不愿改变的麻木，不愿抵抗的麻木。这长**穷**的日子要如何自救呢？不过要**换**着办法吃，吃得有滋有味，吃出不平之气。

回望**红**薯相伴的日子，一共十八年。舌头，**肠**胃已经有了**记忆**，即便不吃**红**薯，只看见了，也能把那味道翻出来。今日笑自己，长得像**红**薯，像**红**薯的外表，呆呆的，拙拙的，笨笨的。心也像**红**薯，生时脆脆的，爽爽的；熟时**软软**的，**热热**的。做人也要如**红**薯，禁得住蒸，禁得住烤，禁得住炒，禁得住压，更要懂得翻身。

《吃咸菜》

有咸菜的日子，算是不**寻**常的。**寻**常的日子，**连**咸菜都没有。咸菜一下肚，压得住**饿**，镇得住胃。有咸菜，**一顿饭**变得厚实起来。有咸菜，**红**薯也吃出"肉味"。母亲总是**说**，你们少吃一点咸菜，咸菜好**贵**的。

家里有个咸菜罐子，罐子大，咸菜少，总是不够吃。一个得意的**萝**卜，被切碎，经过腌制，毫无生气，蔫蔫的。日**积**月累，失去了**鲜**丽的色彩和**圆润**。但吃**饭**时，被盛在一个小碟子里的咸菜，那份神气和尊**严**，那重见天日后的精气神，看上去精致了**许**多，甚至比肉还要精致和珍**贵**。咸菜，好吃在哪里，似乎**说**不出个所以然来。或**许**，在于它的味道吧——"咸"。所**谓**的"味"不过是重**盐**。奇就奇在这个重**盐**的玩意，还**让**人念念不忘，嘴巴总**贪**念它。咸菜吃下去，才有一点**饱**气，不然，胃总是虚空着的。总之，一**顿**咸菜，一**顿**高兴。

那天，我和二哥在家里吃着"**饭**"，所**谓**的"**饭**"就是**红**薯配咸菜。左手拿**红**薯，右手夹咸菜。右手比**较**忙。夹一块，小小的，送到嘴里，"咯嘣"一下。真脆！真香！除了享受咸菜的滋味，还享受嘴巴里发出爽脆的声音。我与二哥**俩**

乐不做声，心里明白，看谁吃的多，谁嚼的声音大。红薯被遗忘了，任它在左手冒着热气。屋里，两人"咯嘣咯嘣"不停。

母亲从厨房里训了出来："别光顾着吃咸菜！三口红薯就一根咸菜，哪有你们这样的吃法！前天才买的，今天就没了。" 我俩不敢吱声，乖乖地吃起了红薯。二哥快快地不说话，怯怯的不敢吃，斜眼瞄着母亲，终了还是忍不住，豁出去，夹起一块咸菜塞进嘴里，一口咬下，"咯嘣"重重的一声，又招来母亲重重的一阵训斥。我听了，不做声，不动声色地往嘴巴里塞咸菜，一块，两块，三块，先含着不咬，然后再吃一口红薯，让红薯在嘴里裹着咸菜，慢慢的咬。嘴巴虽不老实，红薯却是老实的，一点声响都没有，还懂得包庇。如此，吃得并不少，还不被母亲训。不过是换着法子，晃过母亲的耳朵罢了。

我常为自己的小聪明而内疚，为二哥不识大人的眼色而同情。嚼着嘴里的咸菜，望着碗里的红薯，不知道为何，咸菜吃到最后，冒出一阵阵的酸。

《十六棵小桃树》

我家后院有个环**绕**的小土坡，里面种着十六棵小桃**树**。一片天空下，十六棵桃**树**布**满**了枝叶丫杈，**纷纷**联**结**起来庇护我，成了我的天空，任我在里面撒撒欢。旁人看不懂就罢了，**连**我自己也**说**不清在里面到底玩出了什么花样，但我总能在那里一呆，就是半天。我数过多次，是十六棵，那是我童年的憩园。

春，上了枝头，是桃**红**色的。桃**红**色只属于桃，其他的就长不出这样好看的**颜**色。桃**红**点**缀**在长长的，**细细**的枝条上，交枝叠蕊。虽**艳**，但不俗，即便是俗，也俗得**讨**喜。有的盛开了，向天空开去；开了就是笑，在春风里笑。天是一片的**蓝**，桃花在**蓝**空之下，是一朵，是一支，是一束，是一树，是十六棵。上有**蓝**，**蓝**了一片天；下有**红**，**红**了一丛丛。它们相互映**衬**，见了面，相逢了。**红**退了**场**，生了**绿**。叶子**细**长而**绿**，桃是**圆**滚的**绿**。虽是繁茂，但孩子的眼睛天生尖，一眼就能找到**圆**滚的果实。熟了的桃子更是遮不住，总会露出熟的痕迹。**绿中带红**的最好吃。经了春天、夏天和秋天，落了一地的叶子。北风吹来，把褐色的枝条吹成了条条冷峭的雪枝。北风再吹时，有些雪落下，有些雪还挂着。**纷**繁的四季，**纷**繁的桃**树**下，藏匿着一个小小的我，静悄悄的。

桃树园是我的人间。没有一丝威胁，没有一丝酸楚，什么都是风华正茂的。许是我长得小且怕在外受欺负的缘故，总忍不住去关爱和我一样瘦弱的十六棵小桃树。对着与自己差不多年纪的桃树，很是认真，认真得傻，生怕它们饿着，更怕它们死去。它们是我的天堂。在那里，我是"主人"，不是"奴才"，更不是狗崽子。在那里，不必懂事，不必听话，不必受人眼色。打滚，上树，刨土，除草，看书，画画，抓虫子，怎样都可以。大人们说我乖巧，会玩，不闹人。既然他们这样说，我就更乖巧了。我里子也皮，只是"皮"得矜持，"皮"得不出格。有一次，我从一棵桃树上摔下来，不过是伤着了一点皮肉。大哥不问青红皂白把我揍了一顿。我只觉得委屈。这个家中，我是妈妈的宠儿，从无人敢对我动手，只有我大哥打了我一顿。我委屈，又不懂，怎么不但不安慰我还打我呢？我想，只因他是我大哥吧。

那年冬日，我和村里几个小伙伴出去"溜冰"。不料，那水沟的冰面还没有完全结冻，不够结实，走在前面的人一踩，冰破了，一个小伙伴掉到冰窟窿。我的一只脚也插了进去，差点摔个踉跄。幸好，那水沟是不深的。大伙儿合力把我们拉起来，拉出了人，也拉出了一身的淘气。我们又冷，又耽心回家挨打；边走，边寻思如何是好。我提议回我家后院的桃树园，后院的桃树园是我的场子，后院的桃花园是我们的避风港，那里有十六棵桃树帮我们站岗，那里有父亲积攒的柴火，可以生火烤干我们的裤子。三根湿湿嗒嗒的裤腿在火上烤，裤腿冒着气，生着烟，不知谁问了一句："烫到你的鸡鸡没？"

那年盛夏，眼看桃子差不多熟了，我急着把它们从树上摘下来，揣在背心里给母亲送去报功，结果，弄得身上全是桃毛，成了毛猴。皮痒**难**耐，衣服**连带**桃子一起脱去，脱得光溜溜的，洗了个澡。第一次知道那么**圆润**的桃子竟也有欺**负**我的招数。

我的桃花园，一如静悄悄，一个小世界。它**们**听着一切，看着一切，它**们**总是知道我的。

桃园旁的三面是一圈小土坡，土坡斜上方是过去用土夯实起来的寨墙，寨墙环抱着后院，很是厚实。**远远**看去，我家后院的一圈小土坡犹如一座山梁，高高**耸**起。我常常一个人奔跑在上面，登高望**远**。山梁上的风大，天**宽**，地也**阔**。经风吹日晒，小土坡**渐渐**往两边塌了，不如过去高了；但我却高了**许**多。有一次下大雨，雨水往小土坡上的土里**钻**，拉出一道道深深的壕，小土坡的土在慢慢的松，片片的土**顺**着水往两面**倾泻**。我冲到土坡上，**紧紧**地趴在地上，用身子压住土坡，挡住雨水，任雨打在我的身上。我要保护着心中的一片**净**土和家园。我见不得土墙往下塌，见不得好好的一堆土就此冲散。我家已经够破落的了，仅有的一圈小土坡**围**着的十六棵桃**树**，不能再破落了。

殊不知，噩梦还是降**临**了。一天，大队来了几个人，**说**是队里要**烧**窑，需要木材，要把这些**树**都砍去，送到大队。他**们**是大**队**的人，打着大队的名号，**连**斧头都**带**来了，是没有商量的余地了。我心里**顿**时一慌一惊的，呆呆的，一边急，一边哭。母亲见我第一次哭天喊地，又急又心疼。**难为**情地向他**们**恳求："能不能等到明年再砍？"，即便深知大**队**的名义是不可逆**转**的，只是**为**了我，还是拉下**脸**面来求情。眼看斧头一下下落在每一棵桃**树**上，我一边蹭在母亲的后面，一边哭，一边替它**们**疼痛。长起来那样**难**，好不容易长成了一片桃花，还是抵不住斧头的砍。不到两个小时，后院已是一片惨不忍睹的战**场**。这一幕我竟**觉**得在梦里见过。

什么都没了。**树**倒了，天空了，地空了，我的心也空了。哭过，哭累了，痴痴呆呆地站在一旁。什么都没有了，也不再担心失去了，只是从此以后，我再也没有好朋友，再也没人庇护我，想到它**们**被**烧**成灰，堪比天人相隔的**诀**别。我站在原地，对着剩余的幼枝条又哭了一**场**，**捡**起它**们**，**带**着哭腔**问**母亲："**妈**，这些枝可以种**吗**？"，母亲怜惜道："我的儿！别哭了。明年我再**给**你种上。"

第二年，母亲真的种上了十六棵桃**树**。我天天去看，一天看好几回。不知它**们**生了根没？又不能刨开土来看。那些天，我不大愿意吃**饭**，也不大愿意见人，**读书**的心思也没有。迷迷糊糊，朦朦**胧胧**中，想起自己已经失去了的那十六棵小桃**树**，眼角还有泪，落在枕头上。在梦中，我梦见了那十六棵桃**树**，一**阵**尿意，脱了**裤子**，对着它们，滴滴**哒哒**......快点长大吧，我的小桃**树**。

孩童的心本是一**亩**田，种着孩童的梦。我时常庆幸我的童年被这十六棵桃**树**所惊醒，所筑起。虽然，最**终**失去了它**们**，以至于日后，我重新拾起**记忆**的碎片又造了**许多**的梦。我的悲**悯**，我的天真，我的朝气全因**为**它们。我时常追怀童年的忧**伤**与快**乐**，便不断有**爱**意涌出。一片荒凉包裹着一片桃**树**园，一片桃**树**园包裹着一个小男孩，一个小男孩包裹着一**颗**桃般的心。这十六棵桃**树**让我**积**蓄着无**穷**的能量，这份能量**应该**还有另外一个名字，它叫浪漫。十六棵小桃**树**，**让**我一直活在那个十六**岁**......

《此间少年》

年代依然向前，日子依然彷徨，我在生长。

手脚一长，衣**裤**就短了。袖子成了八分的，**裤**管提到了腿肚子以上，鞋底被磨得很薄，脚趾头快要探出来了。衣服、**裤**子、**书**包上留着不少补丁，补丁的样子像把一个**伤**口**缝**合了，看着，还是**伤**。**线**的**颜**色和衣服**裤**子的**颜**色有的一样，有的不一样，瞧着**伤**痕累累的样子。衣服**颜**色也以苦色居多，大多是：灰白，靛**蓝**、黑色。苦中**带**着一股心性，算是硬气吧，不知从何而来，**许**是从地上冒出来的。眼睛里流露的是一股**坚韧**与向上，放着光，似乎使得这个时代**辉**煌了不少。布鞋的底不硬，人**们**的脚步却很硬，总能把地踏起尘土。他**们**扛着**红**旗，吹着哨子，打**锣**敲鼓，昂首挺胸，喊着口号，赶着去开拓新天地。他**们**看起来高亢、激昂，但我一向不喜欢狂**热**的人**们**。

我那时候的样子很是扁平，和旧衣物一样，**缝缝**补补的，穿上破旧的衣服后，样子更蔫了。**饥饿**时常侵**袭**我，步步逼近，我只好**紧缩**肚子。**饥饿**很**难**描述，只要是个人都懂。**饥饿**的索要是不可遏制的，只得由它放肆。成人的**饿**和孩子的**饿**是不一样的，成人只要稍稍一**侧**身，就可以从饥饿的缝隙中逃离，孩子的饿是一种威胁，紧紧被扼住。家中，年幼的妹妹饿的不时哭闹，她一哭闹，我赶紧用红薯米汤之类的喂她。我也很小，但我不能再哭闹了；即便，我也还是个孩子。从小学一年级的时候，我就负责每天去幼儿园接送她，把她背到学校，又把她背回家。可以说是一个孩子背着另外一个孩子。

一晃到了小学六年级。一天下课，班上一女同学在黑板上画了一幅画，画了什么，我记不清了。我站在黑板一旁，比照她所画的，也画了起来。她见我在一旁模仿她的画，立即拿起板擦把她画的抹掉。咦！她生气了么？大约是。我凭着记忆继续画下去。赶巧班主任李老师进来，我握着粉笔，站在黑板前。他看了看黑板上的画，怔了一怔，又看看我，大约不敢相信黑板上的画出自我。当时的班主任是我极喜欢的老师——他姓李，名新。既教语文，又教美术。在我的印象中，他是真的"新"，没有"之乎者也"的老派。他的"新"，带着风，带着光，总让人想靠近。他带着激动和惊喜问我，什么时候学的画画，学了多久了，又赞许我画得好。我当时很慌张，不敢呼吸，整个人僵在那里，口水也不敢咽。

我低声说："老师，我没有学过画画，是照着那位女同学的画的。"我指着她，又不敢正眼看她。

老师接着说："临近国庆节了，每个班级都需要出宣传板报，这期的国庆刊头，就由你来负责"。

我一听，慌乱了，不知如何是好。兴奋之余担心自己做不好，辜负了老师，想推脱，没敢，只说试试。

我恍惚地回到座位上，装作一副听讲的样子，但心思还停在**刚**才发生的事上，在心里一遍一遍地回放。一边招那女孩的**骂**，一边得了老师的关注与**赞许**。心想，若不是她……不断的揣**测**，假设，再假设，再推翻。有点**轻飘**，有点沉重，心**绪**已乱。一切来得太快，**缓**不过气来。事因她而起，不知道是感激还是歉意，更不敢看她一眼了。女孩的伶俐乖**张**，男孩的懵懵懂懂，每个年代，都会有，那不过是少男少女眉目之下的把戏。男孩**们**总会莫名的受到女孩**们**的排**挤**和冷眼；即便是欺**负**和嘲笑，也是一种关注，心里也暗自生出羞喜和跳动。每一次回想起**来**，都如此。

夏夜**笼**罩着大地。人，归了家；鸟，归了巢；还有一些流浪的飞虫和风。夜空中挂着一些星。世界上所有的夜晚，都是相似的。大地一如荒凉，河流一如奔涌。晚**饭**后，老人在屋外摇着扇，**让**自己凉快；坏孩子提着煤油灯抓青蛙，扑在暗处。整个宫家窑只有一、两**盏**灯亮着，等着人**们**都睡去。我还在教室，没有回家。

幽暗的教室，看不见星星是多是少，听不见虫飞与蛙**鸣**。一**盏**昏黄的煤油灯，微微的**闪烁**着。少年赤膊地站在凳子上，稍微一动，凳子就左右摇摆。微微地踮起脚尖，**裤**脚也跟着上去了，提到了脚踝。手**举**画笔，伸着胳膊，上衣被吊到肚**脐**眼之上，露出了扁平的腰肚和**裤**头。忘却了时间，忘却了**饥**渴，忘却了夜的黑与**狞**，忘却了蚊子的侵扰，任它**们**在背上吸噬血肉。整个人**闷**在蒸**腾**的**热气**中，不断冒汗，上唇与**鼻**尖间的汗珠，是微微的咸。夜的暗，始**终**压不住光的亮，越是暗，越是亮。煤油灯向来是脆弱敏感的，一点儿风，就跳跃，摇摆，欲熄不熄。今晚，它默默地燃**烧**，很乖，很安静，好像得到了鼓励，火苗越**烧**越高。到了深夜，火焰稍微不那么兴奋了，平复了，示微了，有点沉沉欲睡。到了后半夜，**渐**入佳境，汗水**渐渐**也收了，开始有了自豪的凉意。

一个教室，一个少年，一**盏**灯，成了一个光与影的**场景**——煤油灯的灯光接近月色光，把夜照得更像夜，把静照得更加静，把人照得更凝神，把教室照得空**荡荡**。那微弱的灯光不那么**开阔**，仅在我身边亮着，其余的地方都是昏暗的。光，照出了明与暗，照出了一个男孩的背景。像是**赞颂**，**赞颂**此刻的虔诚，**赞颂**出一张宁静的画，一幅**伦勃**朗的画，充**满**了**伦**勃朗式的光与影；一尊米开朗基**罗**的雕塑，彰**显**着米开朗基**罗创世纪**的力量。这不过是后**话**。那时候**谁**知道**伦**勃朗？**谁**是米开朗基**罗**？**谁**又能欣**赏**煤油灯的窘境和凄苦呢？一个十二、三**岁**的男孩，手脚、身段**细**幼如枝，没有一**丝**肉感，一**层**薄皮透着骨架，背脊中间凹出一条沟，腰身平扁，肚**脐**小得像只还没有**睁**开的眼。这些，都是不自知的。而我在日后学画中，也未曾作过这幅"自画"，想来，甚是可惜。这又是后**话**了。

这个姿势持**续**了超过十个小时，像是被挂住了。从下午六点到第二日清晨。我从凳子上下**来**，把提在胸口的气，松了下**来**，整个人回过神来，气血慢慢恢复了，才发**觉**双手又酸又麻，肚子空空地叫。回看，空**荡荡**的教室里，只有一排排桌椅齐刷刷地，陪了我一夜。我把煤油灯**给吹灭**了，一股刺鼻的**热**煤油气直冲着我，算是吃了一口油气。天已经大亮了，打开教室的门，清凉的晨风扑面而来，又听见鸟儿的欢声，天边有一点**红色**的曙光。我向着家里跑去，前所未有的**轻快**。

母亲见我回来，十分高兴，**给**我摇扇。定睛一看我，笑了，**说**我的两个鼻孔是黑的。我拿起毛巾，湿了水，往**脸**

上一**铺**，一抹，好凉快，**鼻孔**一挖，一看，果然！毛巾有两处小小的、黑黑的**圆孔**。我自己也笑了。那天的早**饭**和**寻**常日子一样——还是**红薯**，但比以往香甜，**许**是**饿**了。吃得太快，上下都不得，在胸口哽住了，直板板地走到桶边，舀了一瓢水，喝了几口，定了几秒钟，打了几个嗝，才算是通了。有点兴奋。整个人似乎未醒过**来**，通宵达旦的画，有点疲倦，**晕晕**乎乎的，又赶忙回到学校。

听母亲**说**，她好几次来到教室，透过门**缝**，偷偷地看我。**连**脚步都是**轻轻**地，生怕惊着我。透过光，看见我胳膊上、后背上都是蚊子，又着急，又心疼，又不忍打**搅**我，**进退**两**难**，不知道**该**如何。

这算是我有生第一次"做事"，第一次感受到了成就的快**乐**。我等待着事情的发生，也期待老师的"看见"。

老师推开教室门，一眼就看到墙上的刊头，**顿**时，一副不可置信的样子。我**记**得他很激动，我在等待他的激动。他对着我，**说**得很**严**肃："我要告**诉你妈妈**"。我母亲也姓李，也是李家村学校的老师，老师**们**都知道我的母亲，也知道我是"李老师"的孩子。他的**语气坚**定、决**绝**，仿佛事**态严**重，刻不容**缓**。他把学校的**领导**和老师喊过**来**，把我和我画的刊头**赞许**了一番，又向其他老师宣**扬**，这个板报刊头是出自于一个从未画过画的学生之手。

我站在一旁，不做声。他**们**点点头，笑着，不时**转**过头来，看看我，又**转**过去看看那刊头。有的**说**，这孩子从未学过画画，真是青出于**蓝**胜于**蓝**啊。有的**说**，人家还没有出**蓝**就胜于**蓝**了。有的**说**，李老师的孩子就是不一样啊，教育有方啊。有的**说**，这孩子天分好，不学画画，可惜了。他**们**的声音淹没了我。

这是我有生以**来**第一次被关注，被尊重，被肯定。而发**现**我的人正是我尊重的老师，一位"新"老师。我被**骂习惯**了，这一刻**让**我不自在，反倒有种担不起**赞**誉的歉意。在**乡**邻**们**眼里，我不过是一个"反革命的狗崽子"，此刻的"翻身"，**让**我无所适从。那天开始，我原**谅**了西风的荒凉，原**谅**了不可抵抗的**饥饿**，原**谅**了很多歪嘴**恶脸**，原**谅**了十六棵小桃**树**被莫名地遭殃，原**谅**了很多很多。

接下**来**，老师交**给**我一个重任；把全校国庆宣**传**刊头完成，用一个星期的时间。**课**，不必上了。就这样，在校长办公室里**费**时一个星期，从小心到自如；从陌生到熟悉；**进进**出出，出出**进进**。**调**色，画，**调**色，画，一天一幅，一共六幅，最后一天休息。刊头的内容大多数是：天安门、国旗、国徽、**红星**、**红领**巾、**红灯笼**、松**树**等。后来，我看那里都是天安门，国旗，**红星**。

一个星期之后，整个学校、村里、**队**里，都在流**传** "李老师家的孩子是个小画家、小天才"。那段时间，我像是被**烧**着了，不知道哪里**来**的风，一发不可收拾，有燎原之势。我自己也茫然了。在此之前，都是些"孩子事"，懵懵懂懂的，**浑浑**噩噩的。突如其来一束光打在我身上，这道光，好像要把我从命运的角落里揪出来。

自此之后，我便耽溺于画画，画一切能画的，画到天昏地暗。大到天空、土地、河流、山川、村落、房子、人，小至**锅**碗瓢盆、衣服、鞋子、帽子、水**壶**、花、鸟、**树**、虫。画了再画。知道的，不知道的，看见的，想象的。画画就是把活生生的物体"搬"到画本上，我的眼睛和手成了搬运工，眼睛一边揣摸，一边动手画，一刻也停不下来。有时候，眼睛看清了，手却差强人意，没画好。有时候，眼睛半睁不睁，手却很争气，意外的好。比如说吧，画一棵树，假设要把这棵树"搬"到画本上，过去，只知道把树干、树枝、叶子画完，算是完事了，后来比对了一下，发觉不对劲。那棵树是高的？矮的？苗条的？强壮的？老的？少的？枝繁叶茂的？还是秃顶的？朝西长还是朝东长？它的情绪？它的故事？等等。单单一棵树，就够琢磨半天的。琢磨透了，再下笔。眼睛要尖，手也要麻利。画丑了，心里过意不去，觉得对不住那棵树。画得粗率，像干活干了一半，偷工减料。比如说画一片云，那云的飘忽，云的惆怅，晴天的云，阴天的云，有时候云高天阔，有时候乌云压天，那云是低头看着人间，还是闭眼做梦？是想停留，还是想离去？看看天空那云和画本上那云，似乎不是同一片云，笔下的云看似一坨沉甸甸的排泄物。如是，那真的云怕是要生气的。再比如，那人穿了一件花袄子，如何把衣服画在人身上，把花画在衣服上。我看了一眼，画本上那人，衣服不见了，那人身体却长出了一圈的花，快要把人淹没了，不知如何是好，感到难为情。活泼的鸟儿到了我的画上，飞不起来了，像被黏在空中。人在我的画本上好像是扁塌了似的。天空是方，不是真的方；地是圆，不是真的圆。那湾流，那高山，那光景………我小心翼翼地画着，歪歪扭扭的直线，晃晃荡荡的圆圈，每一幅画都是一个踉踉跄跄的我。

我是一个极少发出声响的人。都是静，自己静，做的事也是静的，总不愿制造出声响惊扰别人。当年，年纪轻，不懂"不鸣则已"的心思。后来才晓得，那个夜晚，成了我日后的每一个夜晚。我的人生，也因那个夜晚发生了剧变。北方是不大响雷的，即便在夏日，也甚少听见雷声。之后，我注视着我所注视的，蛰伏于人间，只埋藏一双渴望的眼睛。他们自然是不知道我的底细。

《走出山门》

宫家窑宛如一个罐子，四周被寨墙包**围**，只有一个口。这个口，就是山门。山门，其实没有门。那是一个用土夯实起来的关口，**约**有四、五米高，内壁**约**有两米厚，挖空，成了一座拱形的门。从山门**进**出的人不多，几天才见着一个。山门里面是**贫穷**，出了山门通向的是城市。

那时候，出门要**带**着出门的样子，**进门**要**带**着**进门**的模样。我年**纪**小，除了想当大**队**支**书**的儿子，还有一个愿望，走出山门去城里。

我还未出生时，父母皆是教师，在城里教**书**， 1959年被打成右派下放到农村改造。走出山门，返回城里，成**为举**家的理想。我憧憬城里的光景，是出于孩子的好奇。当时，还不懂事，只是想去城里看新**鲜**，看马路，看火车。出了城，能在同伴面前炫耀。对于母亲来**说**，她太明白，她所担**负**的，所期待的，是一个个子女从山门走出去。

在我上小学五年**级**的时候，大姐**谈**了一个对象，是个城里人。后来，成**为**了我的姐夫。家里有了城里的关系，自然是不同的。**进城**，有了**一线**希望。姐夫是我**们**家中唯一的城里人，也是第一个把我**带进**城的人。

第一次**进**城，像做梦。人小，**年纪轻**，眼睛如何装得下一个城？城的模样就是：人多，车多，灯也多。一条路，十几米**宽**，**乌黑**，笔直，不**转弯**。有的人走左边，有的人走右边，走得很平坦。在城里逛了一天，鞋子上一点泥土都没沾上。我第一次感**觉**，不必太早回家。

从城里回**来**那天，村里人都定定地看着我，好像不**认识**我似的。**进城**回**来**的人，总按捺不住自己的喜悦，在不经意的经意之间炫耀自己出了一趟城，最后弄得人尽皆知。大伙儿拥**围**过来，**问**我城里的光景。过去，我在他**们**面前是个"**孙子**"，**说话**吞吞吐吐的，**结结**巴巴的。从城里回来之后，成了"**大爷**"，**说话**也流利了**许**多。我抖抖身子，定定睛，告**诉**他们，城里的道路是——"玻璃路"。地面是透明的，发着亮，像玻璃一样光溜。他**们**一听，**觉**得不可思**议**，不**说话**了，沉默着，看着地上出了神。又**问**了其他的。我告**诉**他们，火车的速度飞快，像"火箭"一般快。我一边形容，一边指划着天空。大伙儿**顺**着我手指的方向，望向天空出了神，好像在天空里**寻**找火车。我还告**诉**他们：我看了电影。他**们**一听，都兴奋得跳了起来，非得**让**我**给**他**们**演电影。我答**应**着，从家里找来了手电筒，在地里拔了一把狗尾巴草，把他**们带**到我家一个暗的地方。我一手拿着手电筒，照在黑暗的墙壁上，一手**让**狗尾巴草在灯光下甩动着，草的影子落在墙壁上，这就是——"电影"。大家欢呼起来，不断地拍手叫好。自此之后，我有了些"风头"。

记不清距**离**上次**进**城多久，我开始懂事了。听**说**，姐夫这周来家里带我进城。这次进城，可以住上好几天，我兴奋得一夜没睡。这一次，我决心要看得仔细些，真切些。

楼房是楼房，人是人，车是车，没有尘土，干干净净，利利索索的。城里很闹，多是车来车往的声音。依然要去看火车。火车，依然是最大最长的车。我以为没了，还有，还有，还有，不断的，不断的，好长好长，比想象中还要长，　"轰隆，轰隆"地贴在地上前进。一段段的，像是断了，像是连着，太快了，没来得及看明白。要是住在火车边上多好啊，每天能看见火车经过。长大了一定要坐火车，来回地坐。火车是有人驾驶还是无人驾驶？铁路是笔直的还是弯曲的？火车会转弯吗？懂得调头吗？火车会刹车吗？

之后，姐夫带我去了文化宫，那是一个我从未见过的新天地。文化宫好多种画。画有好多种类：国画、油画、素描、速写，素描分人体素描和静物素描。画得好像真的一样。这些纯熟的画技冲击着我。面对突如其来的滋养，我紧紧地看着，想把每一幅画都刻在我的脑袋里。我干涸已久，但凡有些雨露飘来，都能让我贪婪地吸收。直到姐夫喊我三次离开，我才走出了文化宫。又进了新华书店，满室的书香味。书店的书一排排，一层层的，摆的整整齐齐。或是兴奋过了头，像做梦。自己去了哪里，看了什么，也是恍恍惚惚的。只记得姐夫给我买了一些美术书和画画用具，我兴奋得一晚没睡，摩挲了它们一晚。

在城里住了几天，看见城里人有城里人的模样：脱衣，换鞋，挂帽，洗脸，漱口。城里人说话，总不那么着急，不那么大声，慢条斯理的，让人听得明白，听得舒服。吃饭要有吃饭的样子，不能吃出声音，夹菜不能挑捡。姐夫对我是极好的，只是我怕生，不敢乱**说话**。他**们问**我，我就回答，他们若不**问**，我就安静地呆着。环**顾**四周，城里人总会有办法安放自己，安放一切。这是不是他**们**所**说**的——**讲**究。吃**饭**有吃**饭**的**规矩**，坐有坐的**规矩**。客厅里，鞋柜安放着鞋子，拖鞋安放着双脚。厨房里，碗柜安放着碗筷。人与人之间是客客气气的，他**们习惯说**"**谢谢**"。

从城里回来，身上还**飘**着城里的空气，光**鲜**亮丽。我走在路上，想着我所想的，无暇**顾**及他**们**的眼光。大**约**是文化宫展**览**的那些画的**缘**故吧，冲**击**着我，**让**我兴奋又心慌。我想在城里多停留几天，看得再深刻些，再仔**细**些。一方面，又着急回**来**，面对我的画。我有些矛盾，有些沮**丧**。回到家里，我躲在房间里，一遍一遍的回放这些天的点滴。**渐渐**抛开了看火车的兴奋，只停留在文化宫的画和城里人生活方式上的所见所**闻**，一幕幕，一遍遍。我原是个井底之蛙。宫家窑、李家村，不过是一个小井而已。一想到此，我暗自**伤**感。过去我所**认为**的惆**怅**和忧**伤**都不算什么，想起来，它**们**真的很莫名。在心里面挖潜什么，刨除什么，**说**不清，心**绪**有点乱。抬头望望天空，我确信的是我不一样了，天空也不一样了。直**觉**告**诉**我，这次**进**城，不过是**为**以后发生的一切做准备。

回到家里，我决**计为**自己做一双拖鞋。先是找来一条脱了皮的，断裂的皮**带**。把皮**带**剪成两段，比脚前掌略**宽**出一截。削了两个木板，与脚长同等，把它**们**削成差不多脚板的形状，四周磨平整。找来几枚**钉**子，用**锤**子把皮**带钉**在木板的左右两**侧**。**刚刚**好！左右各做一只。一双拖鞋，成了！我**试**了**试**，居然很合脚，只是走起来，有点生硬，像日本的木屐。并非拖鞋不合适我，是我的脚还不适**应**拖鞋。打量起一双自己手工打造的拖鞋，暗自喜**乐**。两只拖鞋仿佛两只小船儿。穿上了拖鞋之后，我才观赏起这双脚，雪白的脚，小小的，还在生长，脚趾头是一个小娃娃，它们是不必懂事的。我想让它们俏皮、生动起来。原来，双脚是可以如此优雅地安放，那是我过去从未留意过的。如此简单，如此不简单。生活原是细碎到不成型的面粉，后来，加了水，变得黏糊起来，再后来，不断搓揉，面粉成了面团，任我们塑造。生活，是想方设法的创造。即便拖鞋不是我创造出来的，但是我的第一双拖鞋是自己创造的。天经地义的创造，天经地义的享受。

穿上新拖鞋后，忍不住往门口走，走得有些摇晃，有些羞涩。爷爷和大伯刚好坐在门口，见我这般，骂了起来。大约骂的是：从城里回来没多久，学上城里人那套，不自知身份，不知天高地厚之类的。又说，穿成这样，如何下田干活，尔尔。两人叨了一会儿。让他们骂去吧，我继续穿我的拖鞋，依然趾高气扬。我的脚趾实在太快活了。他们骂什么，我倒不很在意。我知道，是我刺了他们的眼睛。一双拖鞋，在那时候是奢侈的。人们连奢侈的愿望都不愿意有了。我相信，总有一天，他们也会穿上拖鞋的。

他们以为守旧就是安分。他们极其不喜欢不安分的人和物。他们十分矛盾，自己走不到前面去，也不愿意让别人走到他们的前面去。他们习惯了他们所习惯的一切。若是谁打破了他们的习惯，他们反倒不习惯起来。

我把它们摆放在床底，摆出了一种虔诚。只要一回家，我便第一时间换上拖鞋。生活，已俨然不同。一旦想起床底下有一双自己亲手打造的拖鞋，我觉得，这天有光。

当再次捧着一碗饭时，发现碗边有一圈黑黑的漂浮物，我用手指一捏，手指也沾黑了，看看那炉壁上的黑墙，便明白了，是烟灰。家里少了一个橱柜。我找来了一个**纸**皮箱子和两个木板。木板**夹**着箱子，用**砖**头在两边**稳**固着，如此一来，箱子便不容易移动。再把装化肥的透明塑料袋，刷了好几遍，洗干**净**，晾干，剪开，**钉**在箱子的外面，成了遮挡布。这样，就不会**进**灰了。每次打开碗柜，吃完后，把干干**净净**的碗放**进**去，吃**饭**时，取出干干**净净**的碗，吃着干干**净净**的**饭**。即便碗里装的是**红薯**，但是，那味道和过去已**俨**然不同。

出了山门，**进**了城里，眼界大开。把**该记**住的事情默默的**记**在心里，像藏着一件件心事。我着实变了一个人，变得如何，我也**说**不清。只是，心里多了**许**多山门外的心思。或**许**，他**们**忘了，我是出过山门的人。多年以后，我们家的兄弟姐妹五个，如母亲所愿，一个个都走出了山门。

《老屋》

每回故**乡**一次，见老屋又添了几**许沧**桑和残**败**，心里戚戚然。瓦楞上多了不少野草，风一吹，微微的**颤**抖。久**违**之中的陌生，陌生之中的熟悉。还是那块牌匾——"文魁"和"门有通德"。端端正正，四四方方。这是它永**远**的身份啊，也是宫家的血统和脉搏。我看着它，它也看着我。我**闭**上眼睛，在心里叩拜一声"宫家列位祖先，我回来了。"它默然不**语**，是一种答允。老屋，**终**究是老了。幸好，还**认**得出来；它自然也**认**得出我。

算起来，老屋住了几代人了，**该**老了，已有作古之**态**。门的样子没变，只是旧了，旧成了褐色，木的褐色，还是好看的。**锁**也旧了，生了**锈**，好像**锁**着一个故事。墙边周**围**长了不少**杂**草，草长有人高，几乎淹没了老屋。走**进**屋里，一股**陈**腐的味道，掩埋着故人故事。屋内的摆设所剩无几，空空**荡荡**的，只剩下一些旧得不能再用的**杂**物。屋子很暗，几**缕**光**线**从上面射下**来**，可见灰尘在半空漂浮。哦，是雨水把瓦打穿了。啊！我**认**得出来，这是我的房间。外墙塌了，露出了一个大窟窿，可见**蓝**天。木梁折了下来，瓦和墙塌成了一个土堆。墙外的荒草趁虚而入。天

空，残墙，荒草，旧床，我怔怔地看，这原是一幅油画
《老屋》。

我喜欢旧，一切的旧。说不清的理由。旧，像是失色的**铭
记**，淡化了深刻，成**为**了一种温存，**让**人忍不住走**进**它。
老屋的**颜**色旧的很好看，是失色而已，旧得有故事。只
是，怀旧的人越**来**越少了，愿意听故事的人越**来**越少了。
老屋就是在**讲**一个故事。有些故事，已经**讲**不清了。窗户
落落破破的，只剩下一个窗框子，已没有了昔日的风光。
墙壁斑斑**驳驳**的，墙上有了水**渍**一般的屋漏痕，**讲**着光阴
的故事。堂屋中间摆着一把椅子，已经作古，看一眼，**让**
人惆**怅**。每个角落我都不曾忘怀。小时候，没人**给**我**讲**故
事，我就看这个老屋，它就是一个故事，可是我总猜不透
它在**讲**什么。如今，大概知道了。

我家住在宫家窑的祖宅里，是一座青灰色的**砖**石砌成的院
子。父母**说**，我的老**爷**叫宫玉柱，是清末**举**人。宅门上方
挂着的那副"门有通德"和堂屋挂着的"文魁"牌匾是皇帝**赐**
予的。牌匾斑斑**驳驳**的，黯淡无光，虽风化了不少，但痕
迹依旧清晰。我还未上学，什么字都不**认识**，母亲最先教
会我**认**的就是——"门有通德"和"文魁"这六个大字。我时
常站在堂门前，看着，比划着，好像在看着曾祖父一样。
似乎，他也在看着我。虽然，我未曾见过曾祖父，但是我
想，他一定如这块牌匾一样的老派和**严**正。倘若曾祖父还
在世，他可以教我**读书识**字，也一定最疼**爱**我。

前院住着三**爷**一家子，后院住着我**们**一家子。三**爷**原是我
的亲**爷**；只是，二**爷**没有后，三**爷**在父亲小的时候把他过
继给二**爷**了。二**爷**过世得早，留下了我们一家子和奶奶。
我们有点前后不着岸。对于父亲来**说**，养父过世了，亲爹

隔阂了，到头来，无人接应。三爷是父亲的亲生父亲，应该亲亲亲热热才是，可是，客气中显得不自然。过继了，就有分别心了。亲爹不是亲爹，不知谁是亲爹。奶奶觉得我们是过继的，对我们不温不热。总之，各住各屋，各干各活，各吃各饭，相安无事。

"那宫老爷子人好着呢，对乡里乡亲挺照顾的。几兄弟好像就老二好一些，也是没福的，要是长寿些，怕是还能保得住……"，又接着说："这么多子孙，看上去没个像是宫老爷的眉目。那最小的三尖子，还有点像宫老爷子年轻的模样，尤其那嘴巴，那神态，有几分像，不说话的时候最像。"

他们的同情与叹息，掩饰不了看戏的心情。他们数落着别人家过去的辉煌与今天的残局，像是在评论一场戏一样轻松，戏落幕了，无戏可看，自然是可惜。

我们一家子像是被命运所抛弃的，被时代所清理的，被家族所冷落的一堆陈年旧物，被安置在失落的一角。一代书香世家，好像这座房子一样，灰灰的，旧旧的，落落破破。

虽是窘迫，但，穷有穷的欢喜，再穷，也是要过年的。腊月二十三开始，村里一派忙年的气象。冷空气上环绕着一种欢腾，虽冷得心头紧，却是欢喜的。兄弟姐妹们都放假了，大家不如过去赶忙。大哥和二哥在家修修补补，做些细碎的活儿；大姐围炉打着毛衣；小妹在看书认字。赶忙的依旧是母亲。她把家中的细软全部拿出来洗晒，把脱了单子的棉絮抱上竿上晾着，用擀面棍敲打，一下，两下，三下，上上下下，左左右右，里里外外，细细碎碎的尘埃在阳光下漂浮。母亲落了一身碎絮，她不曾在意；接着，把被套和单子在水里揉搓，敲打，黑黑的灰水，重重的酸楚一阵一阵的被挤压出来。

家家户户的炊烟从早上到晚上不断，整个村子显得很蒸腾。平日里喊我"狗崽子"的乡邻们也慈容了不少，不和我玩的小伙伴们也慢慢地亲近了我。过年，对于孩子们来说是个盼头。盼新衣，盼红包，盼鞭炮，盼好吃的，盼好玩的。

母亲买来最便宜的猪头和猪蹄，单靠这个猪头和猪蹄，她便可做出几套供奉祖宗的供食和支撑一个年关的肉味佳肴。除夕傍晚，父亲张罗着上供神位，大哥在八仙桌写春联，我和二哥爬梯子，贴春联。一张"福"字，正正当当的被贴在门的"额头"上；三张小的春联贴在门的"下巴"，像三根红胡子，飘着，唱着；门的两侧各贴上一张，像是脸颊两边的大腮红。看上去，像一个唱戏的脸面，上了大红的妆。老屋也新了起来，穿新衣，化新妆。大姐帮着母亲下厨，小妹跑前跑后凑热闹。

吃饭了！除夕年夜饭，在远远近近的鞭炮声中，一家子围着一锅热饺子，吃得热腾腾的。碗里的蒸汽把脸都遮盖了，只看见模模糊糊的脸，那热气让每个人的脸变得滋润和光亮，眼睛也湿润了起来。一个个白胖的饺子，里面有点肉，裹着母亲的祝福。我想一口吞下，太烫了，不能。咬上一口，白白的饺子皮有了牙齿的痕迹，肉味的咸香。一个接一个的吃，最后喝上饺子汤，肚子鼓得如饺子。父亲走出屋外，准备生火熬年，我跟了出去。虽然，父亲平时是不作为的，但在除夕晚，那是他的舞台，我便是他的小帮手。有父亲守候的夜晚，这个家稳当踏实了许多。饭后，母亲在房里给每个孩子分着鞭炮、糖果和压岁钱。大家把各自所得放在床头，看着，数着，守着。

对我来说，最开心的事是能穿上新衣服。躺在床上，兴奋得睡不着，朦朦胧胧之间，看见窗外的火，是父亲在守候。窗外的火，烧得通红亮堂，松枝在火堆上"劈劈啪啪"的爆破。一阵又一阵的鞭炮声远远近近传米。这是个不眠的夜。好多故事离我越来越远，甚至，我分不出哪些是真的，哪些是虚幻的。我只想，明早大年初一的第一顿饭不必是红薯。

大年初一，开门，火药味扑面而来，刺鼻却是香的！地上都是被炸开的鞭炮，一地的残红。这就是年。我站在门外，穿着新衣，踩着地上的残红，寻找一些没有被炸开的哑炮。这些哑炮还有未燃烧的火药，只要掰开，点上火，还能出火花。哪怕是这一点点的火花，也能使我欢乐起来。村里头传来鞭炮声、烟花声，断断续续，长长短短，一阵接着一阵。权势人家的鞭炮像个大红的圆饼，圆饼解开，一长串，宛如一条红色的长蛇，在地上蜿蜒。点着火之后，这条红红的地蛇像是着了魔，整个身子在地上乱窜，蹦跳，在地上蹦出了火光和响声，一声接着一声的爆破，快要烧到尽头时的那一声，响得短促又密集，似乎所有的力量都堆积在那里，"轰隆"一声，火力四射，像炸弹一样，炸开了花，在长空中落幕，宣告他们的胜利，宣告他们的圆满。我们家的鞭炮是一封单薄的"小红包"，常常由大哥或二哥掌控，撕开包装，露出火引子，一点，往空中一扔，"噼噼啪啪"几声，落在地上再"砰啪"几下，挣扎几下，冒出一股青烟，没啦。

"来，你们给爷爷拜年，祝爷爷身体健康，给爷爷磕头。"

母亲拉着我们，跪在地上，双手作揖，嘴巴说着过年说的祝福。爷爷坐在椅子上，笑呵着："好！好！好！快长高长大，为宫家争光啊。"爷爷每人发了一个红包。我小心地拆开红包，几个堂兄弟也拆着，他们得了两毛钱的红包，我家的总是一毛。

拜祭了宫家祖先之后，把老屋的门锁上。这时候，天阴了起来，怕是要下雪了。我与母亲准备启程回城。打量起宫家窑，陆陆续续盖起了一些新房子，新的发亮，亮得光鲜，住这里的人也不像过去沧桑了。遇见几个乡邻，他们认出了我和母亲，请我们去家里坐坐，直直地夸母亲会教书育人，每个儿女都出息成才，尔尔，客套。他们看看我，说是认得我，但含含糊糊，说不出名字。过去叫我"狗崽子"的乡邻们都老了。过去的事情，大家都不愿提得仔细。生活改善了，人也善了，气也平了，懂得笑了。相互寒暄几句，道别了。

临别，回望老屋，老屋还是一如的静，静静地听着我们悄悄地回来，悄悄地离去。人一走，老屋就没有多少气息了。我在心里再次向它叩首，它始终默然恪守。它承载了我的出生，我的童年和我的青年。老屋的每一处都藏着我的期盼，我的失落，我的喜悦，我的哀愁，我的秘密，我的追逐。幸好，老屋总有老树相伴；而老树，总会春来发枝生芽，秋时落叶飘零。一片落叶，轻轻的回旋于半空，终落于老屋的墙角上。老屋，总有老屋的归处。

《如是而然 》

知天命之年，总想**给**自己一个**说**法。**终**了，我也只能淡淡
的**说**一句:"如是而然"。

2012 年 3 月 12 日，当我的第四个系列作品"天**问**"(Site 2801)
在美国加州州府美术**馆** Crocker Art Museum 开展后;当我
和我的作品"天**问**"**专题**报道在美国国家电视台 PBS News
Hour   播出后;当我拿到美国国会、加州**议**会、州府市长**颁**
发的荣誉**证书**时;当自己过半的作品被收藏和被**购买**时。
作**为**一个旅美艺术家的我，怎么也激动不起来。我多么眷
恋我**刚**到美国时，心里那种陌生和空空如白**纸一张**的我！
我独坐在工作室，呆望着百年历史的木**结构屋顶**，看着四
壁堆得**满满**的作品和**颜**料，还有**刚**从美术**馆**抱回来的一沓
证书和**鲜**花。似乎，眼前所发生的一切就像一台大戏**刚刚**
谢幕，什么都没有发生，什么都不存在。掌声**让**我重返那
个少年，依恋着我那十六棵小桃**树**和那块小土坡的少年。
我最兴奋的不是掌声的那刻，而是准备，和我准备好的那
刻。我想这是自我的**觉醒—该**向内走了。

回想，在我大半艺术生涯中，总有这样一个怪圈，也几乎
是同样的一幕：每当爬到高处后总想急切的从高处下来。

记得三十年前，我的大学毕业创作"高山巅"荣获河南省大学生美术作品大赛一等奖，作品悬挂在省美术馆展厅的正中央。十年后，再次到广州美院继续深造，一步一个辉煌。我同样也是激动不起来。不记得从什么时候起，我养成了喜欢躲着人群走路的习惯。或许是父母悲惨的政治阴影的影响?还是自己的性格和境况所局限?总喜欢一个人独自走远，又会独自回来;喜欢一个人飞奔在高山之颠，又喜欢摸索在峡谷深处;我好像一直都是一盏鬼火，一盏敢于远离大地，又愿意回头着陆的鬼火。也许，这是命中注定的。

曾记得，在很小的时候，别的孩子都喜欢在街上成群结队的疯跑，我好像总是只能一个人在我家后院守着那属于我的世界：一条长型的小土坡和一块方形的十六棵小桃树园。后来，那十六颗小桃树被村里的干部们硬是给挖走烧啦，仅剩下的那块小土坡也常在大雨中被一点点的冲走，连同我为此常常痛哭的记忆。那是我第一次感知失去和无奈，第一次拥有抱负和力量。也可能是从那时起，我第一次懂得能拥有的仅是自己的思想和行动，而不是外面世间的荣耀和纷争。

这些年，我的每一副画，每一个系列作品;我的每一次触动，每一次灵感，都是源于童年的经历和记忆，青年的体悟和纠结。我不想再执于过去的，现在的，得到的，逝去的，渴望的，唾弃的……恍然，已是个两鬓白发的中年。成长的只是时光，老去的依然是时光，而我，还在那里。人生，破碎的，已破碎;完整的，终会完整;曾经破碎的梦，终究还能圆梦。或"怪圈"或"一幕"，还好，自己的油门和刹车永远都是在自己的脚下。脚似乎是一直朝着前方迈进，但心却每时每刻都回望着过去。

转眼，从那个小土坡跑到了美国加州，一身泥泞，从未妥协。有幸，在知天命之年，可以无忧无**虑**游历于加州和大理，这两个皆可称**为**世外桃源的地方，我尽可以静**为观**止，画心双修。也**许**，这是一个可以**让**我一改前半**辈**子"**为**物所**转**"，而**为**"以我**转**物"的开始吧。承蒙这次出**书**之际，第一次把在美国这十几年所做的东西凑在一起，虽不成体统，但对自己，也算是个梳理;对别人，也就权当穿着便装出门见一次客人。好在，心里踏实，下半**辈子终**可以全心思**继续**艺术这个行当。如是而然。

05/01/2014

186

《春笋》

今天，是正月十五元宵**节**，是我童年**记忆**里过大年的压**轴**戏。

这一天，且不**说**那四面邻村八面庙会的**热闹**，单就母亲在这一天那"大赦"的豪迈和气魄，整整引**领**和影响了我的童年直到今天。

在这一天，母亲**为**了过年所准备拾掇的年**货**供食是决不再看管的，猪头肉伴蒜白菜尽可以大口的吃，烤的焦黄的**红**点白蒸**馍**是允**许**吃**饱**的，对着那保命的**红**薯当然是可以**阔**气的嫌弃一次而无需愧疚的，尤其是父亲总会在这一天取出那套家**传**明代青花茶具，沏上一**壶狮**峰龙井摆设在堂屋八仙桌的中央供全家消食，解渴和品茗一番。

正月十五元宵**节**，我一直是**记**得的，尽管美国这里不过**节**，但这一天，我依然**习惯**着过**节**忙碌的样子。**记忆**中的元宵自然是不易**买**到的，看着初春的街市**刚**出**摊**的**鲜**嫩竹笋，我定下心，今年我要拿竹笋去追**寻**那正月十五吃元宵的**记忆**和情怀。

对竹笋的**记忆**那已是童年以后的事；第一次是十六**岁**后我

看的第一本书，巴尔扎克的《幻灭》三部曲里的《两个诗人》中的一段对白得知，竹笋不是普通百姓能消费得起的一道法国贵族名菜。第二次是进入六十岁之前，偕美院同学陈永忠在江西九江"宋代四大家"之一的黄庭坚的故居，又被誉为"华夏进士第一村"写生时所住的竹林和餐桌上的"土鸡炖竹笋"，才开始对竹笋略懂一二；竹笋，是要春雨过后在次日晨雾采下的竹笋，拿土鸡中火清炖方为上品，那竹笋入口棱角分明，干脆利落，不卑不屈，清口回味。难怪苏东波有"宁可食无肉，不可居无竹。　无肉令人瘦，无竹令人俗。　人瘦尚可肥，士俗不可医。"之精辟卓见。

其实，竹笋并非仅是小说里的一道名菜，更是参禅悉心的一道滋养。

一顿春意快然的正月十五土鸡炖竹笋，在加州阳光的沐浴下，在甜蜜的回忆，思念和新的轰轰烈烈的憧憬中隆重下肚，今年，就这样由竹笋担当主角圆了童年记忆里过大年的这场压轴戏。

02/08/2020

《宴会家猫的遗嘱》

今晚，当我离开宴会时，我的书僮告诉我，宴会家的猫被气死啦，据说是因为我。

这只猫的遗嘱上是这样写的：

我一直远远的盯着那位艺术家，把一条鱼吃的净光。我想，或许他会在鱼骨缝隙间漏下些肉末什么的，待他离席后，我总是可以坐下来，把嘴贴在盘子里或鱼骨间讨些东西出来，也好在我的小弟兄面前炫耀一番。可我怎么都没想到，一粒肉末没剩就算啦，一点腥味都没留下，就连第二第三根尾骨也被偷吃了去。唉，当初，我教老虎时留了一招，不教上树，我的猫氏家族得以世代安平。我和人蜗居时屈尊降贵，拾一些他们剩下的碎鱼肉沫来吃，我的猫氏家族就足可维生。如今，老虎仍一直信守着当初的约定，但人已完全没有当初的人样啦！

如此下去，我的这点智慧是没法子养活我的猫儿们啦，我还有什么脸面去见我的猫氏晚辈呢？

再见啦我的猫儿们！

04/11/2020 老猫于猫工作室

《猫性》

猫的性情孤冷，样子也冷，尤其是鼻子与眼睛，不必靠前去，都能感受到一份阴凉之意。或许是阴凉的鼻端，锐利的眼睛造就了猫的冷意。它们总眯着双眼，对世间流露出一副不屑一顾的神态。

猫的样子告诉世人：懒洋洋的态度未尝不是一种活法。它们常年躲在阴暗处，不大在光天之下走动。猫的面孔相差无几，并不十分好辨认，正如去纽约大街上看人，发现街上的人长得都差不多。我甚少关心猫，猫也甚少关心我，这是何其公平的事。猫比人容易得道，但不要因为猫吃鱼，猫抓老鼠，便认为猫凶残冷暴，况且猫吃鱼，抓鼠是本能，但无碍于它们得道。

我原以为，猫主必定是一位如猫性情之人。后来发现，爱猫人士大抵为同猫性恋者，同乐于孤傲亦惧怕孤寒。也许，这是物以类聚法则吧。猫大约掌握了人心，更掌握了生存的定律：要得宠，要得人心，必须若即若离，不远不近。它们天生懂得用一双无形的猫爪子轻挠人心，这是他们得宠的缘故。

我不曾见过一只**沧**桑的猫，它**们**从不向世人展示**为**生活受
累受**饿**的形**态**。这**让**我想起索居离群的哲学家、艺术家、
文学家，他**们**始**终**是淡漠的，猫性的。他**们**至始至**终带**着
猫眼，**窥**视世间，把世间看得冷，看得薄，看得透。人类
的生活方式与情感形**态**正向猫靠近，人类开始不关心人
类。

《2020中秋》

月**圆**山高银河幽，

寒星已被风吹丢，

荣辱虚华**标善场**，

风自清道水自流；

少年离索世事究，

倦客始知因果由，

故**乡**大洋天地长，

今夜早眠无需忧。

10/01/2020

《圆满》

———

走出文魁门，

告别黄河**谣**，

断离珠江情，

踏过东西桥；

自幼行忠孝，

青春激情**烧**，

践行德业言，

滋养禾田苗；

上住金山**颠**，

鸟瞰银河滔，

朝暮起仙舞，

日月伴我老。

Yuebin Gong

11/20/2020

《今生同乐》

望着**绿**莹莹的山坡，

闻着黄灿灿的花；

蓝蓝的天幺，

清清的河；

六十个春秋幺，

十六**岁**的花；

这是加州阳光，

这是我的家；

这是我们的草地午餐笑声啊！

——我们即兴高歌！

盛起**热腾腾**的饺子，

举起这**满满**的酒；

浓浓的情幺，

慢慢的喝，

六十个日夜幺，

十六**岁**的傻；

这是新的故**乡**，

这是我的家；

这是我们的至亲**挚**友之**爱**啊！

——我们今生同**乐**！

3/16/2022 与**挚**友明东草地午餐感怀

《倘若时间能倒回》

王教授推着位坐在轮椅上的百岁老人，竟在斜坡的人行道上玩起了滑雪的游戏，那架势显然有着一身童子功的样子。

王教授躬着小虎背，撅着小屁股，双脚以外八字交替着往前登，双手紧推着平衡把柄，两道很是泼皮和自信的目光从眼镜片后像箭一般向前射出。轮椅和轮椅上的百岁老人随着向前风驰电闪的速度发出咯咯的笑声。霎那间，王教授果断用力送出飞奔的轮椅和轮椅上的百岁老人，"您也不害怕？您怎么这么有安全感？"，在旁边保驾护航的宫行长看着被送出的轮椅和轮椅上的百岁老人发出惊叫。

轮椅在撒野的飞奔，轮椅上的老人在格格的狂笑。双脚已变换成内八字姿势采取了急撒车的王教授，看着前方经过自己严密数学计算，依靠惯性正在匀速飞奔的轮椅和轮椅上的百岁老人；听着呼啸向前的风，和风与风之间向后传递着轮椅上百岁老人那停不下来的笑声；王教授抹了把额头的汗，盯着前方的速度已开始减缓准备倒回的轮椅和轮椅上的百岁老人，犹如，观察者由地球飞向火星完成太空探测后，自动变档，变速，按照原轨道开始徐徐返回的飞船，，。

"嗨嗨！您真的也不害怕？怎么不想您的轮椅在一直往回倒呀？"，在一旁护航的宫行长**紧张**的提醒着，，。

终于，正在往回倒的轮椅和轮椅上的百**岁**老人，平**稳**滑向王教授用身体和双臂形成的弧形返回基地，轮椅上的百**岁**老人像是被父母高高抛起在空中的宝贝，由惊吓到快**乐继**而欢笑回落在父母的怀抱。

这时的王教授**红**光**满**面，汗珠**顺**着头**顶竖**起来的头发向上**闪烁**着光芒，那一派孩童**习惯**了的，挑战胜利后的神气和喜悦，似乎在告**诉人们**：时间可以倒回。

宫

2021年11月

《给母亲的信》

妈妈：

日里我忙着看**书**没怎么想您，夜里得**来**一遍一遍端**详**着小**伟**发来的您的照片和视**频**，末了，我停留在十月二日小**伟**发来的一个视**频**上，一个我99**岁**高**龄**的母亲像小学生一样摇头晃**脑**在**认**真看着屏幕**读书**的**场**景。我看了一眼时间是凌晨两点半，但我舍不得停下来，舍不得漏掉视**频**里那一**丝**一毫**牵肠**挂肚暖我心**窝**的**细节**。

妈妈，我看着您随着**节**拍起舞的**满**头银发，**紧**扶着桌子有力的双手和有**节**奏踏着地板的双脚；我听着您朗朗的**读书**声　　"好雨知时**节**，当春乃发生，随风潜入夜，**润**物**细**无声，，，"　；我瞧着佩戴耳机端坐在屏幕前，**显**然是一个您昔日所教的**课**堂里最优秀学生模样的您；我想像着二十四小时呵护和陪伴在您身边的女儿和女婿的辛劳，，，。此刻，我想写下，被这世道阻隔在万里之**遥**长达三年的儿子几句心里**话**：**妈妈**！我**为**您在99**岁**高**龄**的今天，仍能保持着您一生所一如既往的年**轻**，激情，毅力和豪迈的精神而感到无比自豪和**骄**傲，同时，我也深深地怀着一**缕难**言的愧疚和不安。

妈妈，每当我们视**频**的时候，您久久地看着我**说**出的第一句**话**总是："看你头发和胡子都白清啦！"。我懂您这句**话**背后的含义和您对我疼**爱**的份量。您是最知道，我是如何从极度**营养**不良**频临**死亡的**婴**儿花去两块五毛**钱捡**回的一条性命，我是如何从**贫穷**不公的**乡**村依靠着艺术学业一步步走**进**城里脱**颖**而出，我是如何信守着初心怀揣着艺术梦想毅然走出黄河，勇敢**闯荡**珠江和登高跨越太平洋。您还**记**得**吗**？因我的乖巧，懂事和"**穷**人孩子早当家"所一路走来的德行，我是我**们**姊妹中唯一一个没有挨过您打的孩子，一晃，我也亦老去。我是知道的，您是如何的集**严**慈合一的母亲。

妈妈，我是多么深深地**爱**着您和我**们**的家才有着永**远**对您**说**不完的**话**呀！

妈妈，您我都老了，我们的头发都白了，似乎我们已都昏昏沉沉不懂世事了，似乎我们两代人都到了偃旗息鼓的时候了，似乎，我们已殚精竭智，但是，我们又奇迹般地同步死里翻身开始了我们新的活法。我想，这是因**为**我们都有着家族血脉所需要的一**颗**年**轻**，激情，毅力和豪迈的精神，作**为**宫氏家族文魁**的**后裔，我想，我们理当如此**继续**我们的使命**顺**世而**为**活出我们新的篇章。我们**证验**了一句俗**话**：百年长勤，智者不懈。

妈妈，您已**树**立起我们新篇章的旗**帜**，您的吃好，睡好，身体好和您天天**读书**，日日健康的精神是我**们**全家的福音。您就这样天天快**乐**的**读书**，做回您最喜欢的学生模样和您昂**扬**挺拔的自己，做回您90年前**为**求学而**绝**食抗争的大户人家的小姑娘吧！

妈妈，时钟已过凌晨四点，顺着这会儿我满腔的暖意，我也向您汇报一下2018那场政治噩梦之后我的顿悟和我的新生。

妈妈，回望我走过的六十年艺术人生，修身三部曲："立德，立业，立言"，对此，我倍感欣慰和感恩。感恩您和时代造就了我一个能竭尽所能全力以赴而为之的自己。当下的我，唯一之兴趣便是想做学问。六十年来我从没有过真正做学问的经历，也不太懂兴趣的真正含义。但当下的我只想学着做学问，或称补学问。何以称做学问为我的兴趣，我想，世界于我已陌生不解，唯"兴趣"是由我自己可以尝试驾驭自养自补的事，是可以淡泊名利、成败、恩怨的事，是无所为而为之当无用之用之事。

妈妈，或许这是我还能做的，或许这亦是我们家的一种福音。

预祝妈妈99岁生日快乐！！！身体健康！！！

您的儿子 小斌

2021年10月18日于美国加州

缀：创伤后艺术家的乌托邦

【创伤后艺术家的乌托邦】的灵感来源于我对小舅所需生活环境的讨论中导出的假想。 虽然假想来源于小舅，但它可以引出适用面极广的一些问题:我们在怎样生活，我们想要怎样生活，我们能控制生活中的哪一部分，我们如何面对掌控之外的生活等等。不过作为一个描述空间和生活概念的假想指南，这个标题有很多需要扩展解释的地方：

【创伤】通常指向一个对人的精神和身体造成打击的事件以及事件的后遗症。但在这里，创伤的概念远远超出了打击艺术家的事件所影响的范畴。它的主体是艺术家当下人生与上一阶段人生之间的对比所造成的心理冲击，这其中既有他身心状态下降后感受到上一阶段"影子"对自己的嘲讽，也有对当下人生感到迷茫时对上一个阶段的浪漫化重构。在艺术家理解和适应自己当下人生之前，这种创伤会如影随形，在他遇到任何或大或小的挫折时都会瞬间现形。只要艺术家在做事，它就有机会从各种琐事的缝隙中钻出来影响他对周遭一切的看法。

【艺术家】在这里并不是指艺术创作者的职业头衔，而是这篇指南对乌托邦里疗伤的人所寄予的期望。这里的人脱离了为生活奔走和为社会创造价值的工作环境，并因为上

面提到的**创伤**而**难**以面对生活或理解社会。这个时候的他
需要将自己重新塑造成一个艺术家:一个用艺术来抹平**创
伤**,面对生活,理解社会的人。这个艺术不再是需要大众
欣**赏传**播出价的雕塑或画作,而是能**让创**作者本人发自内
心去欣**赏**的艺术。它可以是文字研究,视**觉创**作,也可以
是美味佳肴,炉边小酌,甚至可以只是海湾上的朝露晚
霞。最重要的是,它可以**让**艺术家撇下生活**琐**事,全心投
入,不**给创伤**留任何可以发**挥**的机会。

【乌托邦】乍一看似乎并不能准确表**现**这篇指南所描述的
空间,因**为**这个**词**本身更多指向社会**层**面的完美无缺。但
它的孤立和虚幻状**态**恰恰可以表**现**我们想要描述的空间特
质:它自成一套规避了所有矛盾的生活系统,而这套系统
仅仅是**为**艺术家当下**疗伤**的状态而**暂**时存在的,就像早晚
要被骨骼丰**满**的幼鸟**顶**破蛋壳的鸟蛋一样。这个**乌**托邦并
不是一个**现**实生活模式的范本,而是帮助艺术家思考当下
和未来人生的工具。**乌**托邦的本意是一个人人都拥有**满**意
生活的社会**蓝图**,而这篇指南对这个**词**的挪用也**蕴**含了艺
术家在**疗伤**过程中找到自己想要的生活的愿景。

1. 【**创伤**后艺术家的**乌**托邦】坐落在面向海湾的山
    上,用距离把熙熙攘攘的都市推到了地平**线**边**缘**
    背景画的位置,也用高度把近处城镇的存在**缩**减
    成了偶尔迫不得已才会光**顾**的超市银行和寿司
    店。这个位置天然地拒**绝**了艺术家不愿面对的城
    市社会和它代表的大部分生活**琐**事,剩下的那一
    小部分**则**由**乌**托邦内部消解。

2. 艺术家早晨被窗外的鸟**鸣**和水流声**唤**醒,走出房
    间开始晨**练**。与上班族疾行赶路中的被动**锻**炼或

健身者完成**预**定数据的日程性**锻**炼不同，艺术家在晨**雾**和阳光下的每一个动作都在与周**围**的环境对**话**，和空气，鸟**鸣**，水流，花**丛**，甚至**远**处冉冉升起的都市一起构建只存在于早晨的动**态**艺术作品。

3. 一套拳打完，艺术家**转**过身走向厨房，他背后的院子里开始涌**现**出一件接一件的**琐**事:水池清洁，园艺管理，**扩**建改造的**进**度，……但这些都被厨房的玻璃门挡在外面，而艺术家此时正埋头**钻**研他的下一个**项**目:在咖啡，橙汁和煎蛋三明治中**寻**找艺术。这是一个时间跨度只有十分钟的作品，但在艺术家的生涯中不容小**觑**，**毕**竟它面向的客户是每天都在变得越**来**越挑剔的自己。作品出**锅**的同时，餐桌突然**围满**了人，大家欢呼着看着艺术家"布展"，然后坐在面朝海湾的吧台上，边听艺术家**讲**解今天的**创**意**来**源边在惊叹声中品**尝**。看来今天的**创**作非常成功！

4. 离开餐**厅**，艺术家稍作休息，发**现**他最近两周全心投入的大作品已经像昨天消失时的那样出**现**在了工作**场**地，于是他立即起身**进**入工作状**态**。这种一头扎**进**艺术**创**作的激情和**创**作中百折不**挠**的毅力在艺术家过去的**职**业生涯中并不罕见，他曾经长期使用这些品**质**在艺术圈内外成就事业和推**进**生活，但在乌托邦里，事业和生活日程被屏蔽于他的视野之外，**创**作的本**质**便演化成艺术家对自己内心世界的追求和重获信心的工具。在头**脑**风暴和**挥**洒汗水中，艺术家看着自己下一个**伟**大的作品逐**渐**成型。与此同时，作品周**围**逐**渐**浮**现**出一个个人影，他**们来**自艺术家足迹踏过的世界各地，如今聚在作品四周用**赞赏**，不解，抑或是批判的方式帮助艺术家**给**作品定位。在**讲解讨论**和修改中，艺术家似乎找到了**创伤**前叱**诧**风云的自信，离走出**乌**托邦也又近了一步。

5. 突然，艺术家眼前的作品消失在了空气中，他虽然意犹未尽，但看到午餐出**现**在餐桌上，也就意**识**到自己的工作时长和精力消耗确实达到了极限，以至于**乌**托邦不仅仅**暂**停了他的大作品，还剥**夺**了他**创**作午餐这类小作品的权限。酒**饱饭**足后，艺术家躺在长椅上，看着海湾上方被水**雾**抬到半空中的山和划过天空的飞机，感**觉**这幅景象似乎**唤**醒了之前**读**过但没能理解的哲学内容。此时来自他长**辈**，同**辈**，和晚**辈**的哲学老师们接**连**出**现**在院子里，**围**在泳池旁，开始根据此情此景各抒己见。艺术家半**闭**着眼睛，思**维**在各个老师之间跳跃，又偶尔跳出泳池沙龙的圈子，**继**而把新的**问题**代入到**谈话**中。在沙龙**进**入尾声时，艺术家感到自己的精力在**缓**慢回归。"我的大作品到**现**在还没有出**现**，可能对于大作来**说**今天的消耗确实过大了。但是趁着如此精彩的沙龙余**热**，我**现**在的精力至少还够写一章感悟吧。"他一边想着，一边**转**过身，发**现**自己的电脑出现在方桌上，旁边还有一杯上好的**红茶**。于是他坐起身，开始了午后的文字**创**作。

6. 在**键盘**敲**击**中，天色**渐**暗，太阳离海湾对面都市的天际**线**越来越近，艺术家合上电脑，准备出门边散步边消化今天所写的内容。他穿过院子，发**现**水池园艺都已经整理干**净**，茶室工程的**进**度也更上了一**层**。但艺术家并不关心这些，他只知道茶室完工后他将会多一个可以喝茶听风看雨的地方，其中的过程交**给乌**托邦就好。

7. 在散步的过程中，艺术家身边不断有熟悉或陌生的身影出**现**又消失，他看着太阳**坠**向山后，上方的**蓝**色逐**渐**下沉，把太阳残余的金色压倒在山后方。在天空逐**渐**自我统一的同时，大地上开始出**现**点点灯火。这份由天地呈**现**的艺术**给**了他新的灵感。回到**乌**托邦后，艺术家不仅将这份**转**瞬即逝的灵感融入**进**了重新出**现**在工作区的大作品中，还在晚餐**创**作中**进**行了新的**尝试**。

8. 然而基于艺术家目前的状**态**，**乌**托邦并没有**给**他太多的**创**作时间。在窗外的最后一抹**蓝**色被黑夜吞噬的同时，大作品和灯光**连**同**观**看**创**作的人群一起再次消失。艺术家虽然心有不甘，但又马上被旁边大**厅**燃起的炉火和炉台上出**现**的一杯威士忌吸引。他走到炉边，拿起酒杯的同时投影仪在墙上放出了今晚的电影。按照以往的经**验**，他知道自己的作品在明早吃完早**饭**之前不会再出**现**了，于是他彻底把**创**作抛在了**脑**后，在电影剧情中**结**束了今天的艺术生活。

作者的外甥王皓宇

05/01/2021 于加州

《感恩》

沿着"赤道"上的视野和温暖再走60年！

感恩—那60年所沐浴的"南极"光，

感恩—噩梦2018所遭遇的那**场**"北极"寒，

感恩—那黄河珠江太平洋所重**铸**的"轮回"春，

感恩—家族地久天长血脉相**连**所滋养的"磁场"力。

*** *** *** *** *** ***

父亲：宫尚志（1922-1985）教师。

母亲：李云生（1923-）教师，偃师教委**赐**匾两通《教师世家》《十佳母亲》。

老爷：宫玉柱（1867-1919）字砥堂，晚清**举**人， 光**绪**皇帝**赐**匾三通《文魁》《门有通德》《恩同罔极》；河南省，洛阳市，偃师**县**，寇店**乡**，宫家窑村。

外爷：李恒岳（1896-1942），字景白，堂号-**锡**泰恒，商号-花布粮行，民国**乡绅**；河南省，洛阳市，偃师**县**，寇店**乡**，刘李村。

11/22/2020

外爷：李恒岳（1896-1942），字景白，堂号-**锡**泰恒，商号-花布粮行，民国**乡绅**；河南省，洛阳市，偃师**县**，寇店**乡**，刘李村。

十六岁六十

谨以此**书**献**给**我最敬**爱**的母亲！感**谢**母亲和我的亲人朋友
对我的帮助和关心！

宫跃斌

美国加州

2021

About the Author

Artist Gong Yuebin, known for his remarkable contributions to the visual arts world with works like "Site 2801," "Life's Crossroad," "Essence of Tai Chi," and "Ethereal Ink," has recently embarked on a new artistic journey. This shift in focus has led him to explore the realm of literature, where he shares his life stories and experiences from the first half of his life spent across the globe.

Gong Yuebin's artistic evolution highlighted the diverse range of his creative endeavors. Gong Yuebin's journey serves as an inspiration to artists and readers alike, encouraging them to embrace change, explore different mediums, and express their innermost thoughts and emotions through art.